Pre Get Up To Speed 01

PRE GET UP TO SPEED 1
Focuses on a wide range of daily situations
providing learners with the opportunity to deal with and improve
their proficiency and confidence in communicative English.

CARROT HOUSE

CARROT HOUSE

Pre Get Up To Speed 1
© Carrot House

All rights reserved. No part of this publication may be reproduced, stored in a retrieval system, or transmitted in any form or by any means without the prior permission in writing of Carrot House

Author: Carrot Language Lab

Printed: October 2024

ISBN 978-89-6732-141-3

Printed and distributed in Korea
268-20 Itaewon-ro, Hannam-dong, Yongsan-gu, Seoul, Korea

Curriculum Map

Course	Level 1	Level 2	Level 3	Level 4	Level 5	Level 6	Level 7	Text Book
General Conversation	Pre Get Up to Speed 1~2	New Get Up to Speed 1	New Get Up to Speed 2	New Get Up to Speed 3	New Get Up to Speed 4			
	Daily Focused English 1	Daily Focused English 2						
Discussion				Active Discussion 1	Active Discussion 2	Dynamic Discussion		
				Chicken Soup Course				
					Dynamic Information & Digital Technology			
Business Conversation	Pre Business Basics 1	Pre Business Basics 2	Business Basics 1	Business Basics 2	Business Practice 1	Business Practice 2		
Global Biz Workshop				Effective Business Writing Skills (Workbook)	Effective Presentation Skills (Workbook)	Effective Negotiation Skills (Workbook)		
					Cross-Cultural Training 1~2 (Workbook)	Leadership Training Course (Workbook)		
Business Skills			Simple & Clear Technical Writing Skills	Effective Business Writing Skills				
				Effective Meeting Skills				
				Business Communication (Negotiation)				
				Effective Presentation Skills				
					Marketing 1	Marketing 2		
						Management		
On the Job English				Human Resources				
				Accounting and Finance				
				Marketing and Sales				
				Production Management				
				Automotive				
				Banking and Commerce				
				Medical and Medicine				
				Information Technology				
				Construction				
			Construction English in Use 1 ~ 4					
			Public Service English in Use					

※ This Curriculum Map illustrates the entire line-up of textbooks at CARROT HOUSE.

CARROT HOUSE

PRE GET UP TO SPEED 1

Introduction

Carrot House Methodology

Andragogical Approach & Productive English

The teaching of children (pedagogy) and adult learning (andragogy) are distinctively different. Pedagogy is akin to training and encourages convergent thinking and rote learning. It is compulsory, centered on the teacher and the imparting of information with minimal control by the learner. Andragogy, by contrast, is about education as freedom. It encourages divergent thinking and active learning. It is voluntary, learner oriented, and opens up vistas for continuing learning. Adults need to feel independent and in control of their learning. Therefore, Carrot House curriculum is based on andragogy and is designed to encourage learners' participation and engagement by providing more task-based activities and opportunities to frequently interact in the classroom.

People want to achieve communicative competence when they learn other languages. English education in EFL environments has been rather focused on the receptive skills of English—listening and reading—which simply increases learners' knowledge about a language, not the competence of using it. If people are well equipped with productive skills—speaking and writing—they will be competent in English communication.

This is why Carrot House curriculum is designed to enhance learners' productive skills throughout the course. This andragogical approach of the Carrot House Curriculum, which focuses on productive English, will enable learners to achieve communication skills necessary for global competence. Carrot House's teaching philosophy and curriculum combine to provide a "Language for Success" for all learners

Communicative Language Learning (CLL)

This communicative interaction, the essential component of language acquisition, does not occur in a typical, non-meaningful, fun-oriented conversation with native speakers. It occurs in a negotiated interaction through which a well-trained teacher provides the comprehensible input that is appropriate to the learners. The learners, at the same time, actively utilize the opportunities given to them by the teachers.

To this end, the Communicative Language Learning (CLL) method is employed in the field of Foreign Language Acquisition. The CLL method provides activities that are geared toward using language pragmatically, authentically and functionally with the intention of achieving meaningful purposes.

Course Overview

Objectives

PRE GET UP TO SPEED Course Book series are designed to improve proficiency and enhance the confidence of learners' communicative English in the areas of listening, speaking, and comprehension. The Books focus on a wide range of topics to provide learners with the opportunity to deal with language and themes that a native speaker would face on a daily basis.

Lesson Composition

Pre Get Up To Speed 1 consists of 16 lessons and 8 review activities. Each lesson consists of 9 sections.

1. Getting Started

This two part activity is designed to stimulate the learner's thinking through picture description and situation related questions, and put them at ease in an English speaking environment.

PRE GET UP TO SPEED 1

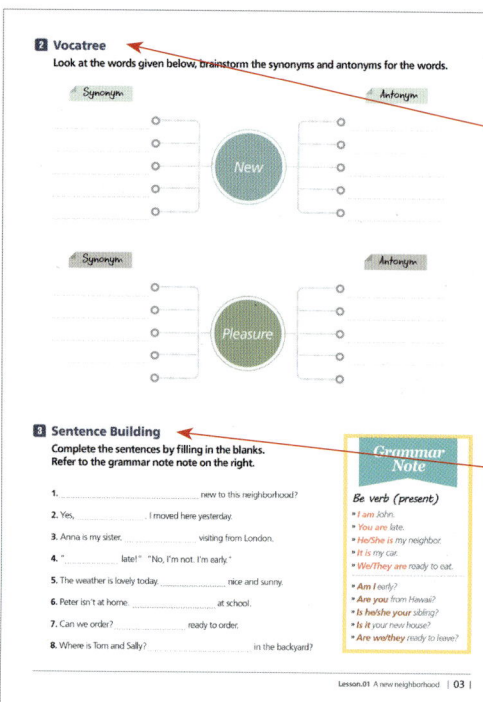

2. Vocatree

Gives learners the chance to expand their vocabulary through brainstorming the synonyms and antonyms of key vocabulary.

3. Sentence Building

Provides an overview of the grammar used in each lesson along with a sentence building activity to practice the lesson's grammar.

4. Dialogue Practice

This section provides a conversation based on the topic of the lesson which includes the key language patterns for learners to practice and understand native English speaking style. Audio scripts and Mp3 files provided.

5. Story Board

Uses visual materials describing two different situations for learners to practice the language patterns of the lesson.

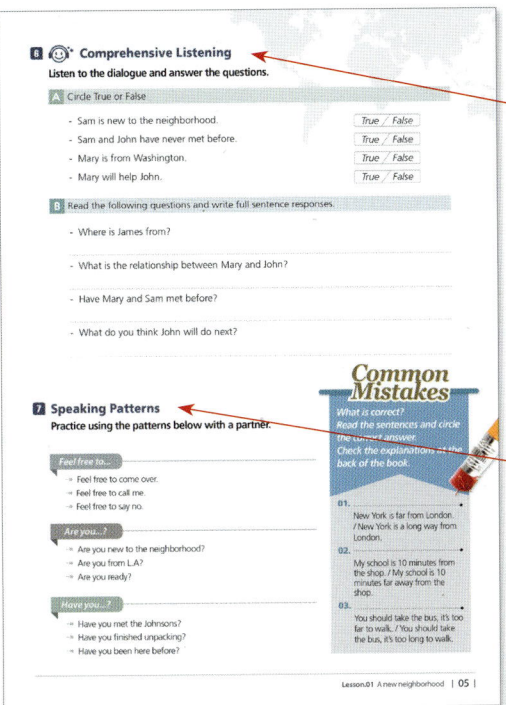

6. Comprehensive Listening
Extended dialogues and questions to provide learners with an area to expand on their listening and comprehension skills. Audio scripts and Mp3 files provided.

7. Speaking Patterns
Acts as a practice ground for reinforcing topic based useful daily expressions and patterns through substitution drills.

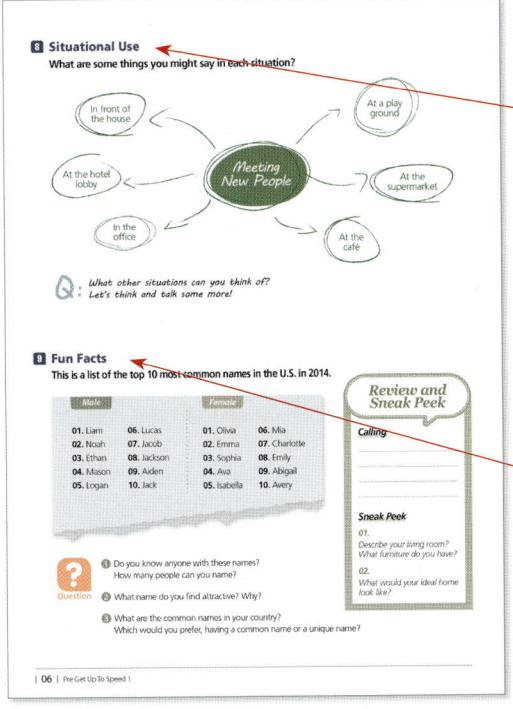

8. Situational Use
Topic guided speaking practice for learners to utilize the language patterns and grammar learned in each lesson.

9. Fun Facts
Presents interesting facts for learners to reflect upon and express their own opinions.

CONTENTS

Unit.01

Lesson Title	Learning Objectives	Speaking Practice	Grammar Note	Page
Lesson.01 A new neighborhood	- introduce yourself and greet new acquaintances - use the "be" verb to ask and answer questions	· Feel free to… · Are you…? · Have you…?	Be verb (Present)	10
Lesson.02 Where can I put this?	- help others arrange furniture in a home - use prepositions of place to describe the location of object	· Put it… · Could you help me…? · Where does…go?	Prepositions of place	15
» Review 01				

Unit.02

Lesson Title	Learning Objectives	Speaking Practice	Grammar Note	Page
Lesson.03 It's a house warming party	- make small talk when entertaining guests at a housewarming party - provide answers to questions using the simple present tense	· Would you like…? · I'm impressed by…. · Tell me more about….	Simple present tense	21
Lesson.04 This is my favorite song!	- discuss likes and dislikes - explain your personal preferences using adjectives	· What did you think of…? · I thought…was great! · Did you enjoy….?	Adjectives	26
» Review 02				

Unit.03

Lesson Title	Learning Objectives	Speaking Practice	Grammar Note	Page
Lesson.05 You look tired	- ask and answer questions about things you did recently - use past tense verbs to answer questions	· I…after work. · We met for… · How was your…?	Past tense (verbs)	32
Lesson.06 I'm running late	- discuss different times of the day - use time-telling techniques to talk about being punctual	· What time is…? · I think it will take…. · I'm worried I'll be late for….	Telling the time	37
» Review 03				

Unit.04

Lesson Title	Learning Objectives	Speaking Practice	Grammar Note	Page
Lesson.07 What are you doing?	- discuss what you and others are doing - use the present continuous to ask and answer questions about current actions	· When are you…? · I'm just… · Are you…tonight?	Present continuous wh- questions	43
Lesson.08 Let me check my schedule	- describe daily routines - use the present continuous and simple present tenses to tell people about your current routine	· I always…after work. · We are planning to…this weekend. · I often…during my lunch break.	Present continuous and Simple present tense	48
» Review 04				

Unit.05

Lesson Title	Learning Objectives	Speaking Practice	Grammar Note	Page
Lesson.09 **Going to work**	- talk about occupations - use simple present tense wh- questions to ask others about their work	· I work as a (an)…. · In the future, I'd like to…. · What does…do?	Simple present tense wh- questions with "do"	54
Lesson.10 **Weekend plans**	- discuss future plans in detail - use "be going to" and "will" to inform others about your plans	· This weekend, I'm going to… · I will…for you. · Tonight, I will….	Future tense with "be going to" and "will"	59
		» Review 05		

Unit.06

Lesson Title	Learning Objectives	Speaking Practice	Grammar Note	Page
Lesson.11 **These are my hobbies**	- discuss your hobbies in detail - use gerunds to describe your favorite activities	· Have you ever tried…? · I enjoy…in my free time. · I find….	Gerunds -ing form	65
Lesson.12 **I've been playing for a while**	- talk about your favorite hobbies and sports - describe the length of time you have done activities using the present perfect tense	· I have…since I was 12 years old. · I have been playing…. · My brother has…for almost 15 years.	Using present perfect tense with "for" and "since"	70
		» Review 06		

Unit.07

Lesson Title	Learning Objectives	Speaking Practice	Grammar Note	Page
Lesson.13 **Can you? Can't you?**	- talk about your abilities and talents - use "can," "have to," and "able to" to describe your capabilities	· I have to…for work. · I can…well. · When will you be able to…?	"Can" vs. "have to" vs. "able to" discuss talents and ability	76
Lesson.14 **Would you like to…?**	- invite someone to do something - use verbs to politely make, accept, and decline invitations	· If you have time, would you…? · I'm sorry, but… · Do you want to join us for…?	Verbs for invitations	81
		» Review 07		

Unit.08

Lesson Title	Learning Objectives	Speaking Practice	Grammar Note	Page
Lesson.15 **Where is the menu?**	- order food at a restaurant - use "I'd like" and other polite phrases accurately in a restaurant	· Could I get….? · I want to eat…. · Could you refill my…?	Phrases for ordering food	87
Lesson.16 **Shall we have some dessert?**	- order additional food and request the bill - use countable and uncountable nouns accurately when discussing food	· We're ready for…. · Please bring me…. · I'd like to order…to go.	Countable/ Uncountable nouns	92
		» Review 08		

Lesson 01
A new neighborhood

Learning Objectives: *After studying this lesson, you should be able to …*
- ☑ introduce yourself and greet new acquaintances
- ☑ use the "be" verb to ask and answer questions

1 Getting Started

A | Look at the picture and describe what you can see.

Tongue Twisters

Practice the tongue twister with your partner.
Who can say it faster?

» Three gray geese in the green grass grazing. Gray were the geese and green was the grass.

B | Read the questions below and discuss with your partner.

① When was the last time you moved somewhere new?
② How do you feel when you go somewhere new?

2 Vocatree

Look at the words given below, brainstorm the synonyms and antonyms for the words.

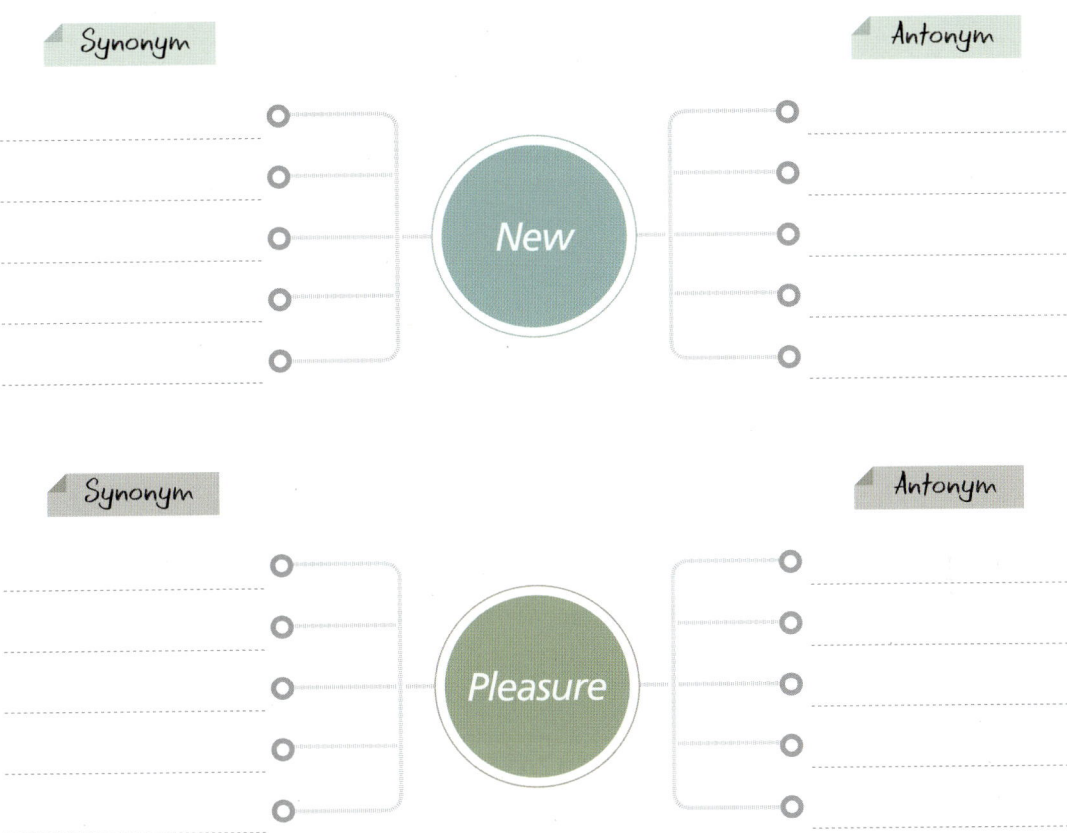

3 Sentence Building

Complete the sentences by filling in the blanks.
Refer to the grammar note note on the right.

1. _____ new to this neighborhood?

2. Yes, _____. I moved here yesterday.

3. Anna is my sister. _____ visiting from London.

4. " _____ late!" "No, I'm not. I'm early."

5. The weather is lovely today. _____ nice and sunny.

6. Peter isn't at home. _____ at school.

7. Can we order? _____ ready to order.

8. Where are Tom and Sally? _____ in the backyard?

> **Grammar Note**
>
> **Be verb (present)**
> » **I am** John.
> » **You are** late.
> » **He/She is** my neighbor.
> » **It is** my car.
> » **We/They are** ready to eat.
>
> » **Am I** early?
> » **Are you** from Hawaii?
> » **Is he/she** your sibling?
> » **Is it** your new house?
> » **Are we/they** ready to leave?

4 Dialogue Practice

Sam : Hello! Are you new to the neighborhood?
I haven't seen you around before.

John : Yes, I am new here. My family moved here yesterday.

Sam : Great! Nice to meet you. I'm Sam.

John : My name's John. This is my family.
My wife's name is Suzie, and this is my son, Zach.

Sam : It's a pleasure to meet you. Are you from L.A?

John : No, we are from Washington.

Sam : Really? Have you met the Johnsons?
They are from Washington, too. Well, we live next door.
If you need any help, feel free to come over.

John : Thanks very much.

Comprehension Questions

1. When did John move to his new neighborhood?

2. What relationship do John and Sam have?

3. Where do you think this conversation is happening?

5 Story Board

Look at the situation and complete the conversation.

6 Comprehensive Listening

Listen to the dialogue and answer the questions.

A Circle True or False

- Sam is new to the neighborhood.   True / False
- Sam and John have never met before.   True / False
- Mary is from Washington.   True / False
- Mary will help John.   True / False

B Read the following questions and write full sentence responses.

- Where is James from?

- What is the relationship between Mary and John?

- Have Mary and Sam met before?

- What do you think John will do next?

7 Speaking Patterns

Practice using the patterns below with a partner.

Feel free to...
- » Feel free to come over.
- » Feel free to call me.
- » Feel free to say no.

Are you...?
- » Are you new to the neighborhood?
- » Are you from L.A?
- » Are you ready?

Have you...?
- » Have you met the Johnsons?
- » Have you finished unpacking?
- » Have you been here before?

Common Mistakes

What is correct?
Read the sentences and circle the correct answer.
Check the explanations at the back of the book.

01.
The woman wanted to buy an umbrella. / The woman wanted to buy a umbrella.

02.
The student wanted to work at an NGO. / The student want to work at a NGO.

03.
There is an university in the city. / There is a university in the city.

Lesson.01 A new neighborhood

8 Situational Use
What are some things you might say in each situation?

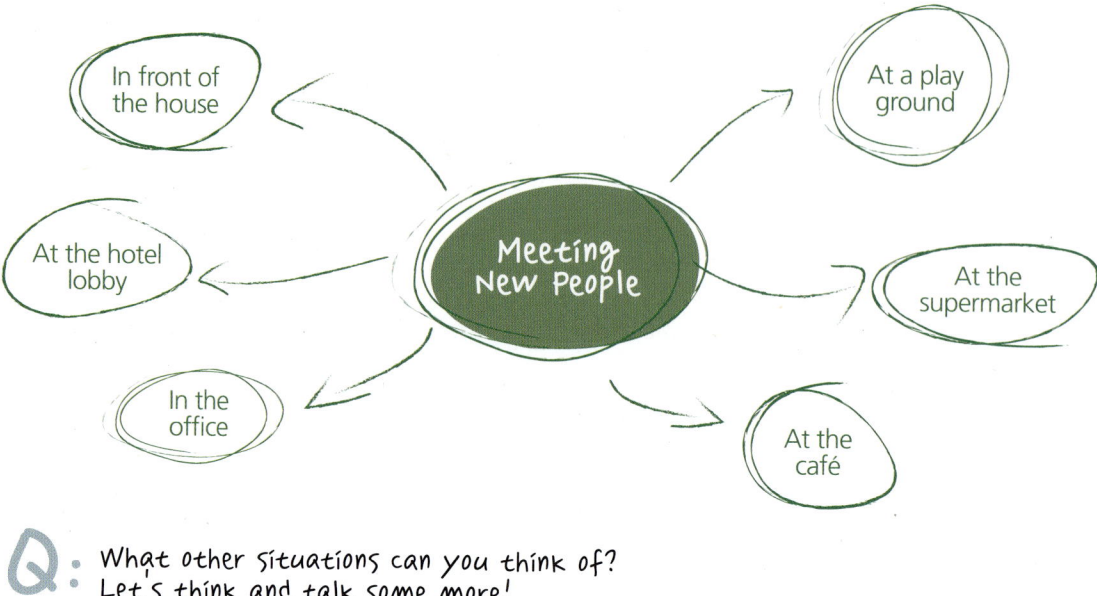

Q: What other situations can you think of?
Let's think and talk some more!

9 Fun Facts
This is a list of the top 10 most common names in the U.S. in 2014.

Male		Female	
01. Liam	06. Lucas	01. Olivia	06. Mia
02. Noah	07. Jacob	02. Emma	07. Charlotte
03. Ethan	08. Jackson	03. Sophia	08. Emily
04. Mason	09. Aiden	04. Ava	09. Abigail
05. Logan	10. Jack	05. Isabella	10. Avery

Question

❶ Do you know anyone with these names? How many people can you name?

❷ What name do you find attractive? Why?

❸ What are the common names in your country? Which would you prefer, having a common name or a unique name?

Review and Sneak Peek

Calling
_____
_____
_____
_____

Sneak Peek

01.
Describe your living room? What furniture do you have?

02.
What would your ideal home look like?

Lesson 02: Where can I put this?

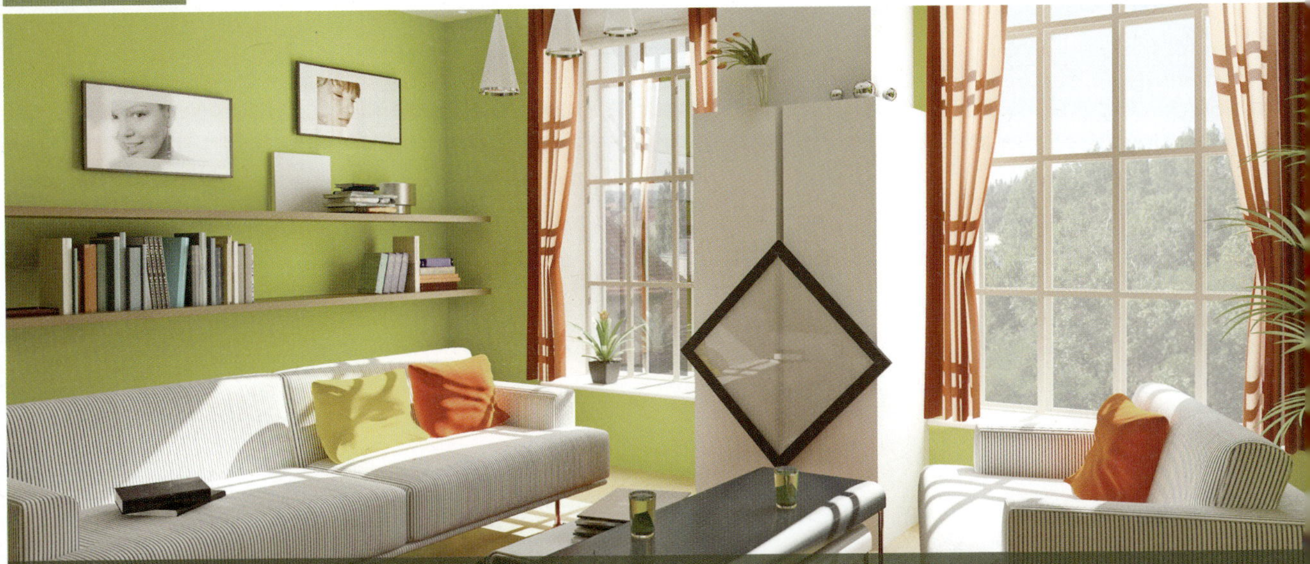

Learning Objectives: After studying this lesson, you should be able to ...
- ☑ help others arrange furniture in a home
- ☑ use prepositions of place to describe the location of objects

1 Getting Started

A | Look at the picture and describe what you can see.

Practice the tongue twister with your partner. Who can say it faster?

» A good cook could cook as many cookies as a good cook who could cook cookies.

B | Read the questions below and discuss with your partner.

1. What furniture do you have in your home?
2. How would you describe the style of your home interior?

2 Vocatree

Look at the words given below, brainstorm the synonyms and antonyms for the words.

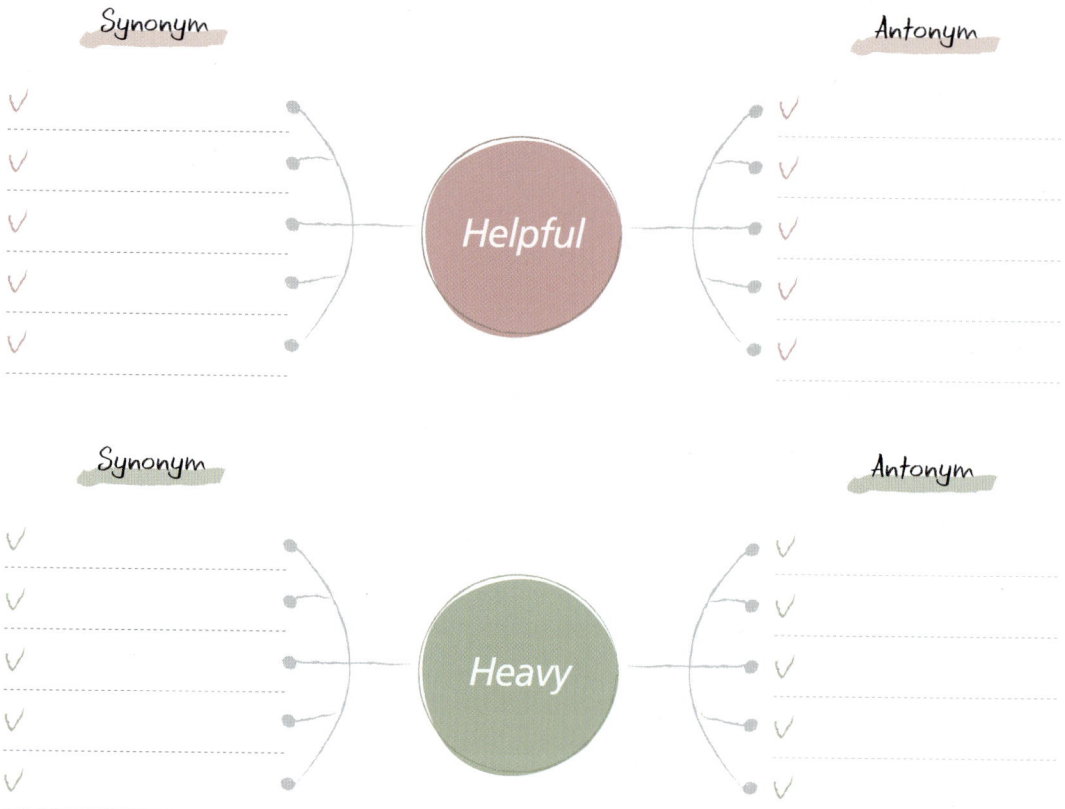

3 Sentence Building

Complete the sentences by filling in the blanks. Refer to the grammar note on the right.

1. I put the book _____ the desk.

2. Could you put my bag _____ the door?

3. I couldn't find the paper, because it fell _____ the sofa.

4. Help me move the bed _____ the window.

5. Put the box _____ the table, so we have more space.

6. I want the couch _____ the two windows.

7. Put the table _____ the dining room.

8. Set the television down _____ the table.

> ### Grammar Note
>
> **Prepositions of place**
> » Put the phone **by** the window.
> » The book goes **on** the table.
> » Set it down **next to** the door.
> » I set it **under** the table.
> ------
> » What goes **in** the kitchen?
> » I think your coat is **behind** the table.
> » The sofa will look good **between** the two tables.
> » I want to put the desk **in** the bedroom.

4 Dialogue Practice

May	:	Thank you so much for helping me move.
Susanna	:	No problem. I'm always happy to help.
May	:	Where does this box go?
Susanna	:	Put it in the bedroom.
May	:	Could you help me move the sofa?
Susanna	:	Sure. Where should we put it?
May	:	I'm not sure. How about the living room? What do you think?
Susanna	:	I think it would look good between the two tables.
May	:	Good idea. Let's move it on three.

Comprehension Questions

1. Whose house are they in?
2. What do they put in the living room?
3. What might they move next?

5 Story Board

Look at the situation and complete the conversation.

Situation.01

Where do you want this table?

Situation.02

The sofa goes in the living room. Put it in front of the window.

Lesson.02 Where can I put this?

6 Comprehensive Listening

Listen to the dialogue and answer the questions.

A Circle True or False

- They are moving a bed.   True False
- The man is Sarah's father.   True False
- The man is moving the desk.   True False
- Sarah likes the bed by the door.   True False

B Read the following questions and write full sentence responses.

- What is the relationship between the two people?

- Where does Sarah want the desk?

- Why do they move the desk again?

- Where is the desk now?

7 Speaking Patterns

Practice using the patterns below with a partner.

Put it...
- Put it in the living room.
- Put it over there.
- Put it next to the window.

Could you help me…?
- Could you help me move the table?
- Could you help me pick this up?
- Could you help me find my book?

Where does…go?
- Where does the television go?
- Where does this table go?
- Where does the box go?

Common Mistakes

What is correct?
Read the sentences and circle the correct answer.
Check the explanations at the back of the book.

01
That apple looks delicious.
Could you pass me the apple?
/ That apple looks delicious.
Could you pass me an apple?

02
A children can be very naughty.
/ The children can be very naughty.

03
The milk is sold in the supermarket.
/ Milk is sold in the supermarket.

8 Situational Use

What are some things you might say in each situation?

Q: What other situations can you think of? Let's think and talk some more!

9 Fun Facts

10 facts you didn't know about chairs.

1. The oldest known chairs were ceremonial furniture from ancient Egypt 5,000 years ago.

2. Chairs came into common use in the 16th century. People sat on benches or stones before that.

3. The word "chair" came from "cathedra," a Latin word that combined words meaning "sit" and "down."

4. A "cathedral" was named after the seat or chair of a bishop.

5. There is no mention of chairs in the Bible, but Shakespeare mentioned them eight times in *Henry VI Part III*.

6. Thomas Edison invented the electric chair in 1889 to show the dangers of electricity.

7. Emperor Menelik II of Abyssinia bought three electric chairs and turned one into a throne when he realized that Abyssinia had no electricity.

8. Benjamin Franklin once said, "The discontented man finds no easy chair."

9. The earliest known reference to the game Musical Chairs dates back to 1877.

10. On December 5, 1854, Aaron Allen of Boston, USA, was granted a patent for his "Improvement of Self-Adjusting Opera Seat," which is the seat that we see at the movie theaters.

Question

❶ Among the 10 facts above, which one do you find most interesting? Why?

❷ Name all the different kinds of chairs you can think of and their usage.

❸ Talk about the chair of your dreams. You can talk about a chair that already exists, or you can create one. Describe its main features.

Review and Sneak Peek

Calling _____

Sneak Peek

01. Have you been to a housewarming party? What was it like?

02. What is a good present for people moving into a new home?

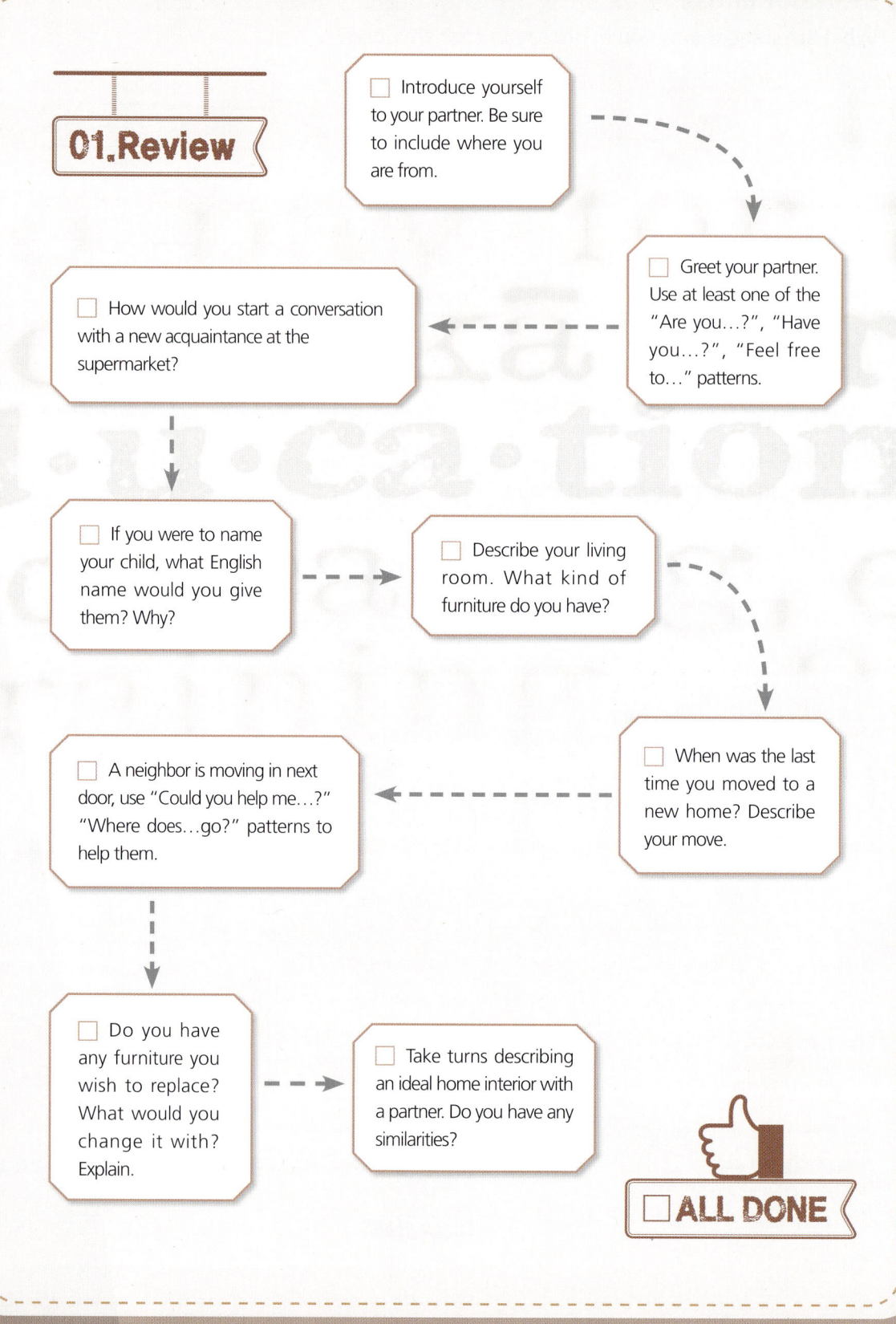

Lesson 03 It's a housewarming party

Learning Objectives : *After studying this lesson, you should be able to …*
- ☑ make small talk when entertaining guests at a housewarming party
- ☑ provide answers to questions using the simple present tense

1 Getting Started

A | **Look at the picture and describe what you can see.**

Tongue Twisters

Practice the tongue twister with your partner. Who can say it faster?

» Black bug bit a big black bear, but where is the big black bear that the black bug bit?

B | **Read the questions below and discuss with your partner.**

① What was the most memorable party you ever attended? What made it special?

② If you could host a party, what would you prepare?

2 Vocatree

Look at the words given below, brainstorm the synonyms and antonyms for the words.

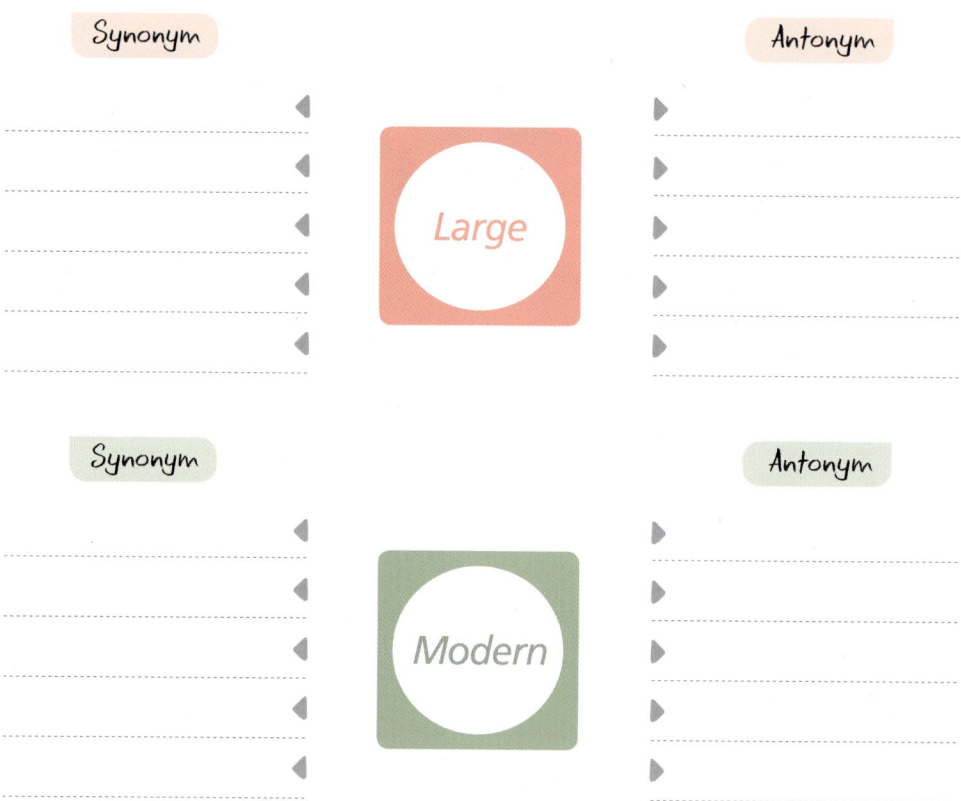

3 Sentence Building

Complete the sentences by filling in the blanks with the correct verb form. Refer to the grammar note on the right.

1. Your new apartment _____ (feel) so big!

2. I _____ (drive) to the office from here.

3. My brother _____ (go) to school down the street.

4. The view _____ (look) amazing.

5. She really _____ (like) the coffee table.

6. You _____ (seem) happy with the new place.

7. I _____ (move) every two years for my job.

8. Your home _____ (look) beautiful.

Grammar Note

Simple present tense

» I **like** the view.
» Your new apartment **looks** nice.
» The room **seems** huge!
» The place **feels** modern.

» I **take** the bus to work.
» My mother **lives** near here.
» I **play** tennis near here.
» He/She **loves** this neighborhood.

4 Dialogue Practice

Jane : Thank you for inviting us to your housewarming party, Alex.

Emily : Your new home is lovely, and everything looks so modern.

Alex : I'm just happy you came. Would you like a drink?

Jane : Just some water, please.

Emily : I'm impressed by the view.

Alex : Yes, it's my favorite part, too.

Jane : Could you tell me more about why you moved?

Alex : Well, I'm actually closer to my work now.

Comprehension Questions

1. Where are they?

2. Why did Alex move? Have you ever moved for the same reason?

3. What does Emily think of the apartment? What style of house do you prefer?

5 Story Board

Look at the situation and complete the conversation.

Situation.01

We're so happy you came to our party. Would you like anything?

Situation.02

Your apartment is beautiful! It has such a lovely night view!

6 Comprehensive Listening

Listen to the dialogue and answer the questions.

A Circle True or False

- The woman is moving soon.   True / False
- The woman lives in a house.   True / False
- The man and woman live together.   True / False
- The apartment is in a good location.   True / False

B Read the following questions and write full sentence responses.

- Where are the man and woman?

- What does the man like about the apartment?

- How many rooms and bathrooms does the apartment have?

- What do you think is a good location?

7 Speaking Patterns

Practice using the patterns below with a partner.

Would you like…?
- » Would you like a drink?
- » Would you like a tour?
- » Would you like to sit down?

I'm impressed by…
- » I'm impressed by the view.
- » I'm impressed by the location.
- » I'm impressed by your home.

Tell me more about…
- » Tell me more about why you moved.
- » Tell me more about your new job.
- » Tell me more about your home.

Common Mistakes

What is correct?
Read the sentences and circle the correct answer.
Check the explanations at the back of the book.

01
James and me are going fishing.
/ James and I are going fishing.

02
I bought the coffee at a café.
/ Me bought the coffee at a café.

03
My friends and me want to eat pasta.
/ My friends and I want to eat pasta.

8 Situational Use

What are some things you might say in each situation?

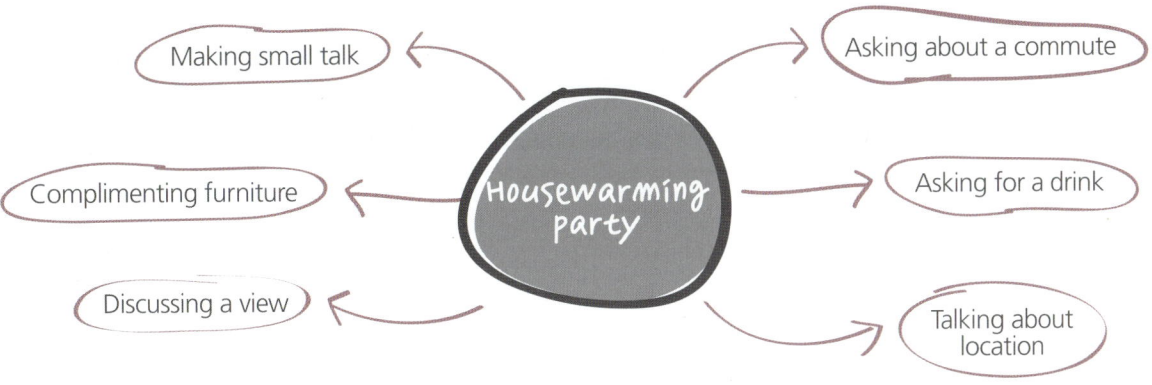

Q: What other situations can you think of?
Let's think and talk some more!

9 Fun Facts

Housewarming Party Games

1. Scavenger Hunt

The scavenger hunt is a fun game to show your guests the layout of your new home. Hide clues and treasures throughout your home and split your guests up into teams to complete the hunt. Make sure to have a good prize on hand for the winning team!

2. Rotating Tour Guide

This game helps your friends get to know your new home while also giving you a little break! You lead the first group of guests on a tour of your home, and then pick a member of that group to act as a tour guide, and so on, until everyone has received a tour. You'll be surprised how much fun people will have while showing off your home, and you'll be free to stick by the door and greet people as they arrive.

Question

❶ Which game do you think would be suitable if you were hosting a housewarming party? Why?

❷ In your country do you have any common party games?

❸ Create a game for a housewarming party. Explain the rules and how to play it to your partner.

Review and Sneak Peek

Calling

_____

_____

_____

Sneak Peek

01.
What kind of music do you like? Explain.

02.
Do you have a favorite musician?
What kind of music does he or she make?

Lesson.03 It's a housewarming party

Lesson 04
This is my favorite song!

Learning Objectives : *After studying this lesson, you should be able to …*
- ☑ discuss likes and dislikes
- ☑ explain your personal preferences using adjectives

1 Getting Started

A | **Look at the picture and describe what you can see.**

Practice the tongue twister with your partner. Who can say it faster?

» I have got a date at a quarter to eight; I'll see you at the gate, so don't be late.

B | **Read the questions below and discuss with your partner.**

1. Give a list of your favorite things. What do you like and dislike?
2. What do you think your preferences tell you about your personality?

2 Vocatree

Look at the words given below and brainstorm the synonyms and antonyms for the words.

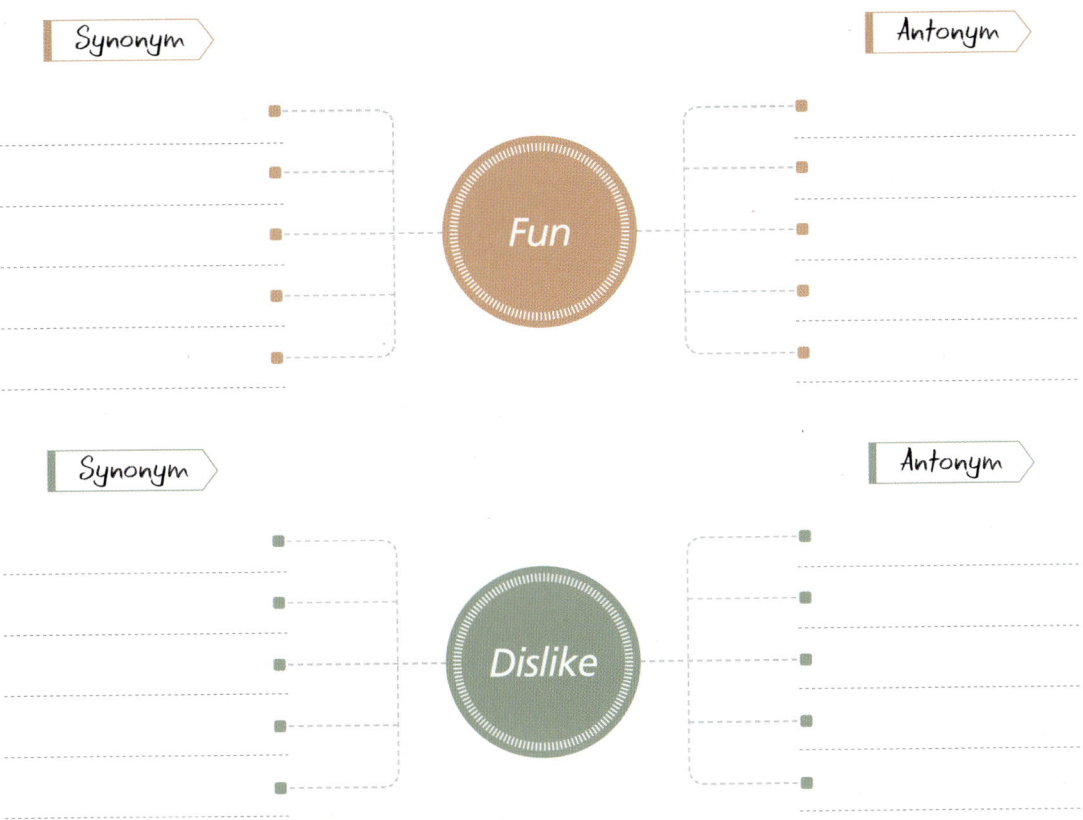

3 Sentence Building

Complete the sentences by filling in the blanks.
Refer to the grammar note on the right.

1. This is the most _____ pie I've ever eaten.

2. The soup is too _____. Could you warm it up?

3. The chicken tasted _____. I loved it.

4. I loved the concert. It was so _____.

5. Your dress is very _____.

6. Tell Bill about your job. It's so _____.

7. I like this coffee shop. The interior is very _____.

8. I didn't know you were such a _____ cook! This is great!

Grammar Note

Adjectives
» I love this **spicy** soup!
» This room is **great**!
» I had a **wonderful** time last night.
» This pizza is very **delicious.**

» The restaurant was **perfect**.
» I dislike **scary** movies.
» Your presentation was **impressive**.
» This cake is too **sweet.**

Lesson.04 This is my favorite song! | 27

4 Dialogue Practice

Marianne	: What did you think of the movie?
Sam	: I loved it. I thought it was great!
Marianne	: It was such a fun movie.
Sam	: The ending was a big surprise. It was so exciting.
Marianne	: I thought so, too.
Sam	: I think it is my new favorite movie.
Marianne	: Did you enjoy the main actor's performance?
Sam	: I thought he was amazing!

Comprehension Questions

1. What were Sam and Marianne doing?
2. What did Sam think of the movie?
3. How was the movie's ending? What genre do you think the movie was?

5 Story Board

Look at the situation and complete the conversation.

Situation.01

Did you enjoy your meal?

Situation.02

What do you think about watching this one?

6 Comprehensive Listening

Listen to the dialogue and answer the questions.

A Circle True or False

- The woman liked the man's kitchen.   True / False
- The man went to the woman's party.   True / False
- The woman is a good cook.   True / False
- The man and woman are married.   True / False

B Read the following questions and write full sentence responses.

- Who had a party?

- What does the man dislike about parties?

- What did the woman make for the party?

- What might the man choose to do after the party?

7 Speaking Patterns

Practice using the patterns below with a partner.

What did you think of…?

- » What did you think of the movie?
- » What did you think of the wedding?
- » What did you think of my pie?

I thought…was great!

- » I thought the play was great!
- » I thought dinner was great!
- » I thought your speech was great!

Did you enjoy….?

- » Did you enjoy the concert?
- » Did you enjoy your vacation?
- » Did you enjoy your meal?

Common Mistakes

What is correct?
Read the sentences and circle the correct answer. Check the explanations at the back of the book.

01.
They gave us the prize.
/ They gave we the prize.

02.
Our mothers and we are going shopping.
/ Our mothers and us are going shopping.

03.
Us boys will go for a swim.
/ We boys will go for a swim.

Lesson.04 This is my favorite song!

8 Situational Use

What are some things you might say in each situation?

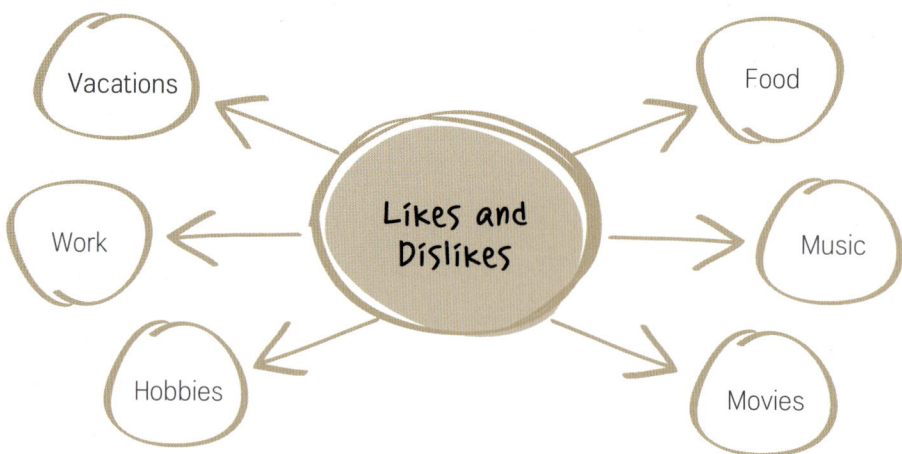

Q: What other situations can you think of?
Let's think and talk some more!

9 Fun Facts

Brand value of the top 10 fast food brands worldwide in 2023.

The graph shows the value of the world's top ten fast food brands in 2023. McDonald's is in the lead with the highest value of $191,109 million, and Starbucks comes next with $61,534 million

❶ Which brand has the highest value, and which one has the lowest? What could be some reasons for the difference?

❷ The chart shows how well-known these brands are around the world. Which of these brands is the most popular in your country? Do any of the values surprise you?

❸ Work with your classmates and brainstorm a list of the most popular brands in your country. What do you think makes them so well-liked?

Review and Sneak Peek

Calling

_____
_____
_____
_____

Sneak Peek

01.
What do you usually do in your free time?

02.
When might someone be tired?

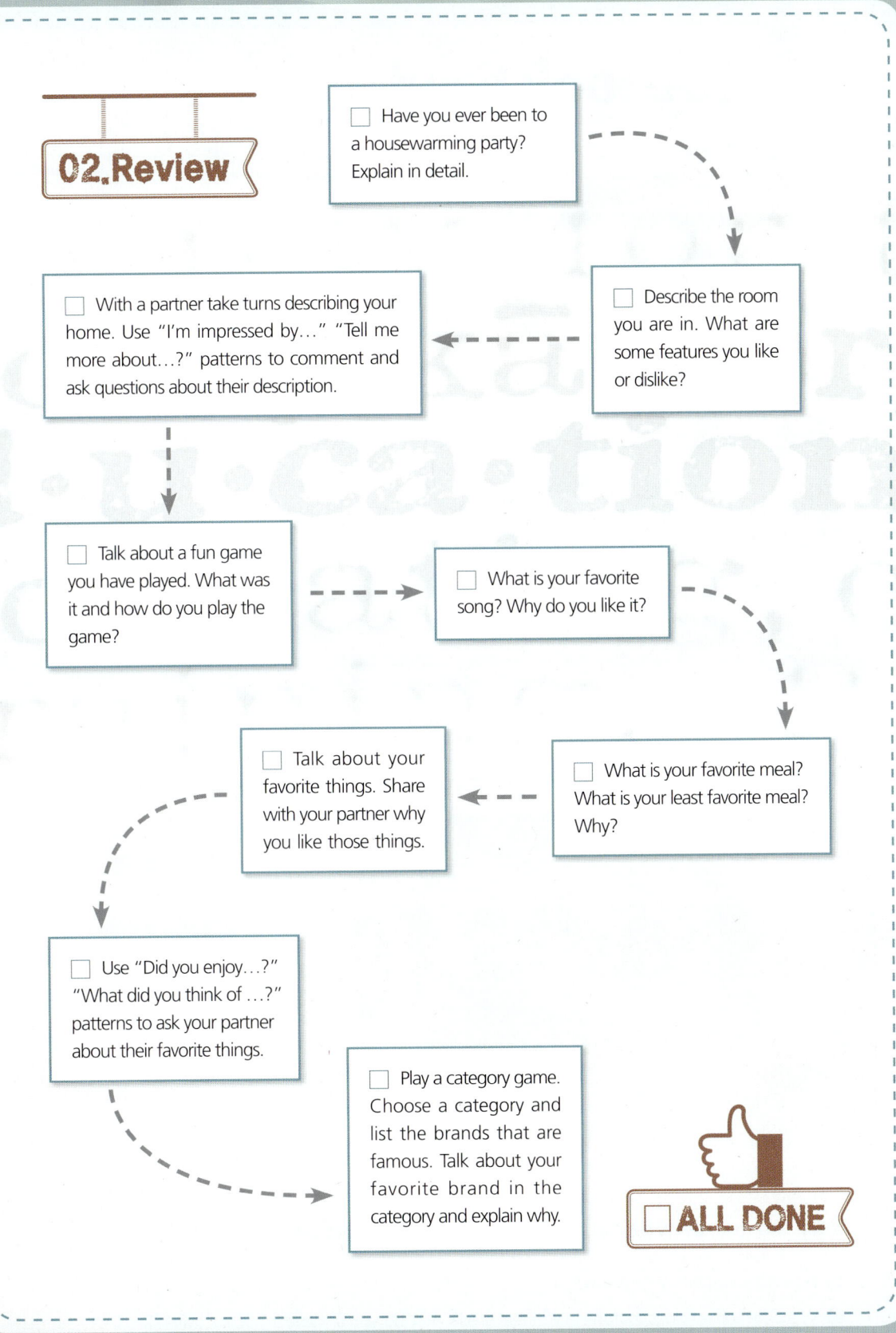

Lesson 05
You look tired

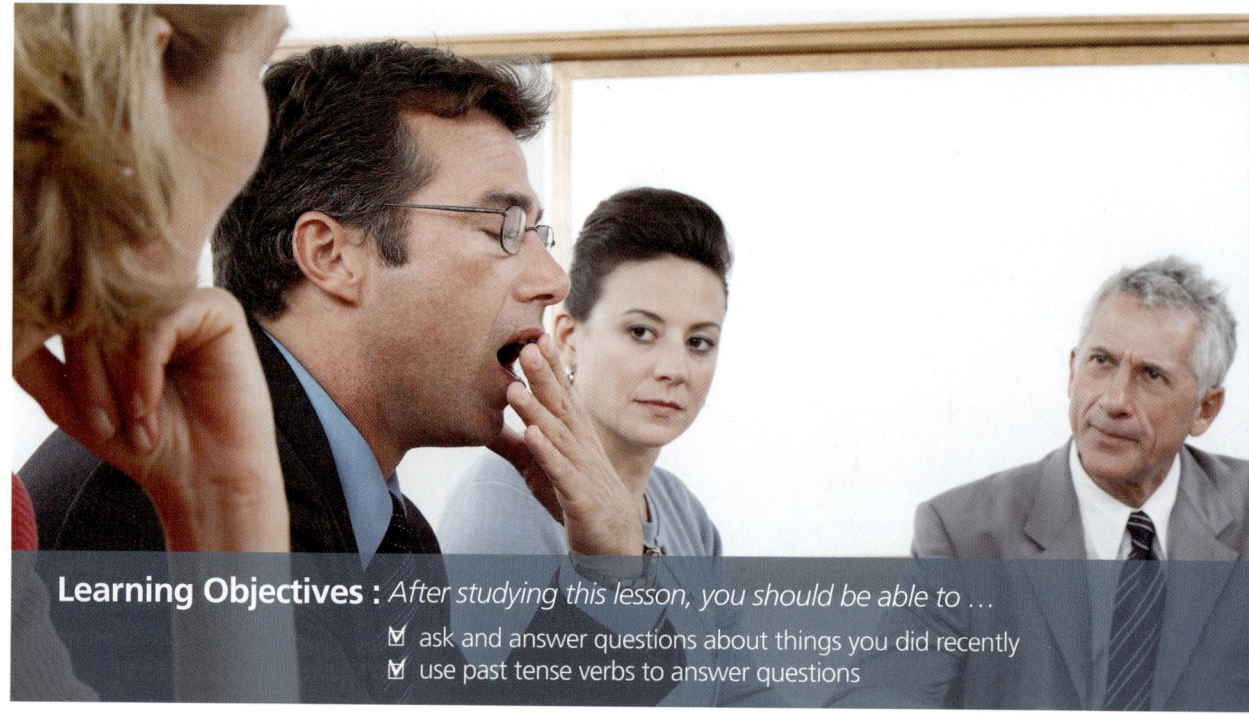

Learning Objectives : *After studying this lesson, you should be able to …*

☑ ask and answer questions about things you did recently
☑ use past tense verbs to answer questions

1 Getting Started

A | **Look at the picture and describe what you see.**

Practice the tongue twister with your partner. Who can say it faster?

» If two witches would watch two watches, which witch would watch which watch?

B | **Read the questions below and discuss with your partner.**

❶ How do you spend your evenings?
❷ What are some things that make you feel tired? Why do you partake in such activities?

2 Vocatree

Look at the words given below and brainstorm the synonyms and antonyms for the words.

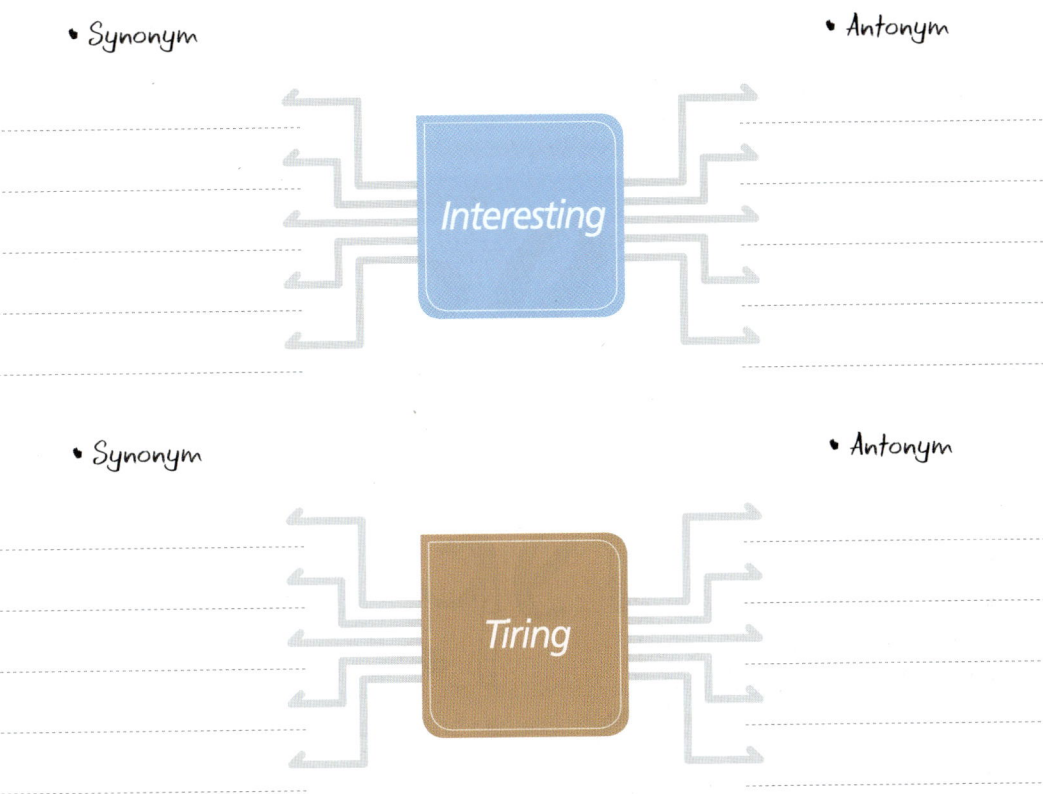

• Synonym   • Antonym

Interesting

• Synonym   • Antonym

Tiring

3 Sentence Building

Complete the sentences by filling in the blanks.
Refer to the grammar note above.

1. Last Sunday, I _____ to the park.

2. After dinner, I _____ television.

3. I _____ my friend for coffee.

4. My brother and I _____ my grandmother.

5. What _____ you eat last night?

6. I _____ my room last night.

7. My mother _____ breakfast for us.

8. My friend _____ me home after the movie.

Grammar Note

Past tense (verbs)
» I **went** to the movies.
» What **did** you **do** last night?
» He **visited** my house.
» I **cooked** dinner for my friend.

» Where **did** you **go** last weekend?
» We **watched** a movie together.
» I **met** my boyfriend.
» I **prepared** for my presentation.

4 Dialogue Practice

Andrew : Hi Michelle, how was your weekend? Did you see Carol?

Michelle : Yes, I saw her after work. We met for dinner.

Andrew : What did you eat?

Michelle : We went to a nice Italian restaurant.

Andrew : That sounds like fun.

Michelle : The food was so good! Do you like pasta?

Andrew : Yes, I do.

Michelle : We should go there together next time.

Comprehension Questions

1. What are they talking about?
2. Who did Michelle meet?
3. Where do you think Michelle and Andrew will go the next time they meet?

5 Story Board

Look at the situation and complete the conversation.

6 Comprehensive Listening

Listen to the dialogue and answer the questions.

A Circle True or False

- The woman went to Europe. | True / False |
- The woman is very tired today. | True / False |
- The man went to Spain after work yesterday. | True / False |
- The man should go home early. | True / False |

B Read the following questions and write full sentence responses.

- Why haven't the man and woman seen each other in a while?

- Are the man and woman married?

- What did the man do after work yesterday?

- What do you think the man will do tonight?

7 Speaking Patterns

Practice using the patterns below with a partner.

I…after work.
- I met a friend after work.
- I went home after work.
- I watched a movie after work.

We met for…
- We met for coffee.
- We met for dinner.
- We met for drinks.

How was your…?
- How was your weekend?
- How was your night?
- How was your vacation?

Common Mistakes

What is correct?
Read the sentences and circle the correct answer. Check the explanations at the back of the book.

01.
Your writing will improve if you practice. / You're writing will improve if you practice.

02.
I hope your feeling better. / I hope you're feeling better.

03.
You're late today. / Your late today.

8 Situational Use

What are some things you might say in each situation?

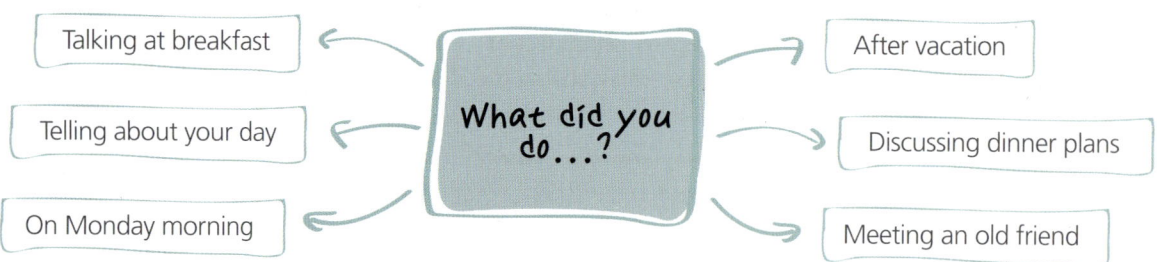

Q: What other situations can you think of? Let's think and talk some more!

9 Fun Facts

Best Time-Travel Movies

1. **Planet of the Apes** is an American film that shows a world where humans and intelligent apes fight for control. The 1968 film adaptation, Planet of the Apes, was a big success, and was followed by four sequels between 1970 and 1973: *Beneath the Planet of the Apes, Escape from the Planet of the Apes, Conquest of the Planet of the Apes,* and *Battle for the Planet of the Apes.*

2. **Star Trek IV: The Voyage Home** is the fourth and perhaps most beloved film in the Star Trek series. The crew of the Starship Enterprise travel back in time to save the humpback whale from extinction.

3. **Midnight in Paris** directed by Woody Allen is a romantic comedy that conveys the message that those who long for the past may be restless and unhappy in the present.

4. **Back to the Future** is Robert Zemeckis' 1985 notable film. It presents humor as well as a heartfelt examination of family relationships.

5. **The Time Machine** is credited with the concept of time travel by using a vehicle that allows an operator to travel purposefully and selectively.

6. **The Terminator** is a science fiction action film, directed by James Cameron, based on the story of machines traveling back to the past to prevent events occurring in the future.

Question

1. The six movies listed above all have the concept of time travel. What of these movies have you seen? What other time travel movies have you seen? Describe your experience of watching a time travel movie.

2. If you could time travel, would you travel to the past or to the future? Why?

3. Share an event from your past. If you could travel back to your past, would you change something? How would you change it? What results would you expect from the change?

Review and Sneak Peek

Calling

_____
_____
_____
_____

Sneak Peek

01.
Are you ever late? What do you say?

02.
When is it important to be on time? Explain.

Lesson 06 — I'm running late

Learning Objectives: *After studying this lesson, you should be able to …*
- ☑ discuss different times of the day
- ☑ use time-telling techniques to talk about being punctual

1 Getting Started

A | Look at the picture and describe what you can see.

B | Read the questions below and discuss with your partner.

1. Are you good at being on time? What are some things you do to stay on time?
2. What are some excuses you can use when you're running late?

Tongue Twisters

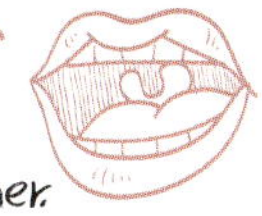

Practice the tongue twister with your partner. Who can say it faster?

» Picky people pick Peter Pan peanut butter. It is the peanut butter picky people pick.

2 Vocatree

Look at the words given below, brainstorm the synonyms and antonyms for the words.

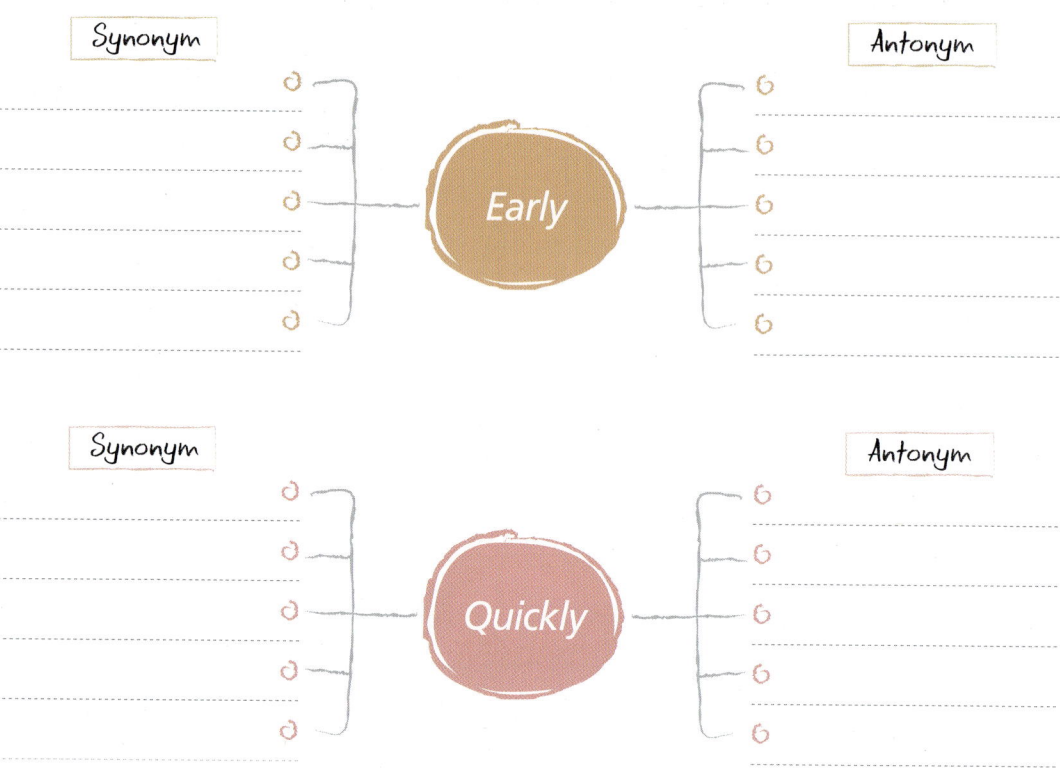

3 Sentence Building

Complete the sentences by filling in the blanks. Refer to the grammar note above.

1. What _____ does the train leave?

2. It starts at 9 _____ .

3. We'll leave at 9 o'clock in the _____ .

4. _____ will you come to work?

5. The dinner starts at 8 at _____ .

6. What time _____ it in New York?

7. My appointment starts _____ 12.

8. We'll get there _____ 5 o'clock.

Grammar Note

Telling the time

» What **time** is your appointment?
» It starts **at** 2 P.M.
» What time **is** it now?
» It's 2 o'clock **in the afternoon.**

» Let's meet at 9 **in the morning.**
» **When** will you arrive?
» I'll arrive **around** 3.
» It's 6 o'clock **at night.**

4 Dialogue Practice

Mark : What time is your dentist appointment tomorrow?

Anna : It's at 8 A.M. I'm worried I'll be late for it.

Mark : I think you should set your alarm extra early.

Anna : That's a good idea.

Mark : When do you think your appointment will finish?

Anna : I think it will take about an hour.

Mark : That's not bad. Do you want me to wait for you?

Anna : That would be great. Thanks.

Comprehension Questions

1. Who will set his or her alarm extra early?
2. How long does Anna expect the appointment to last?
3. What are some things that Mark can do while waiting for Anna?

5 Story Board

Look at the situation and complete the conversation.

Situation.01

What time is it? I'm worried I'll be late for my meeting.

Situation.02

How long will we have to wait? It looks really busy.

Lesson.06 I'm running late

6 Comprehensive Listening

Listen to the dialogue and answer the questions.

A Circle True or False

- The flight leaves at 11:40.   True / False
- The couple will leave at 3 P.M.   True / False
- They are worried about being late.   True / False
- It will take two hours to get to the airport.   True / False

B Read the following questions and write full sentence responses.

- What is the couple talking about?

- Why are they leaving early?

- How far away is the airport?

- What time does the flight leave?

7 Speaking Patterns

Practice using the patterns below with a partner.

What time is…?
- What time is the appointment?
- What time is the movie?
- What time is the reservation?

I think it will take…
- I think it will take 90 minutes.
- I think it will take around an hour.
- I think it will take half a day.

I'm worried I'll be late for…
- I'm worried I'll be late for the meeting.
- I'm worried I'll be late for work.
- I'm worried I'll be late for my flight.

Common Mistakes

What is correct?
Read the sentences and circle the correct answer. Check the explanations at the back of the book.

01
Do you know who's going to speak? / Do you know whose going to speak?

02
I know a woman who's children study there. / I know a woman whose children study there.

03
Who's side are you on? / Whose side are you on?

8 Situational Use

What are some things you might say in each situation?

- Making plans
- On vacation
- Asking about plans
- Making a schedule
- Apologizing for being late
- Before work

Talking about the time

Q: What other situations can you think of? Let's think and talk some more!

9 Fun Facts

Quotes on Punctuality

I never could have done what I have done without the habits of punctuality, order, and diligence, without the determination to oncentrate myself on one subject at a time.
- **Charles Dickens**

I am invariably late for appointments—sometimes as much as two hours. I've tried to change my ways, but the things that make me late are too strong, and too pleasing.
- **Marilyn Monroe**

I am always late on principle, my principle being that punctuality is the thief of time.
- **Oscar Wilde**

Punctuality is the politeness of kings.
- **Louis XVIII of France**

Question

1. Choose a quote which you can relate to. Why do you agree with it?
2. What is your own opinion on punctuality?
3. Use a personal experience to explain how you feel about being on time. What was your experience?

Review and Sneak Peek

Calling
_____
_____
_____
_____

Sneak Peek

01.
What are you doing later tonight?

02.
What do you have planned for the weekend?

Lesson.06 I'm running late | 41

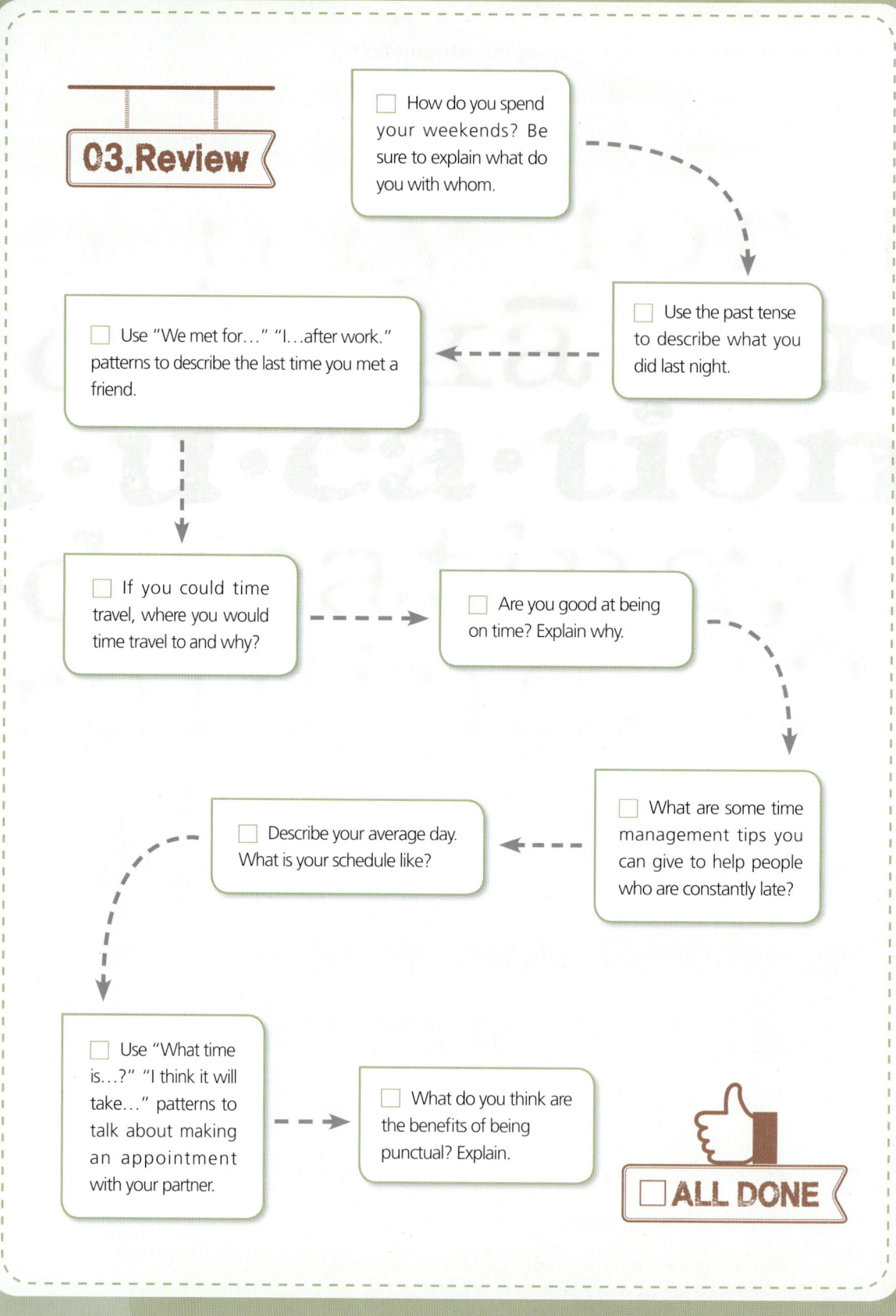

Lesson 07
What are you doing?

Learning Objectives : *After studying this lesson, you should be able to …*
- ☑ discuss what you and others are doing
- ☑ use the present continuous to ask and answer questions about current actions

1 Getting Started

A | **Look at the picture and describe what you can see.**

Practice the tongue twister with your partner. Who can say it faster?

» Love's a feeling you feel when you feel you're going to feel the feeling you've never felt before.

B | **Read the questions below and discuss with your partner.**

① How do you spend most of your time during the week?
② What would you prefer, spending time with many people, or by yourself? Explain why.

2 Vocatree

Look at the words given below, brainstorm the synonyms and antonyms for the words.

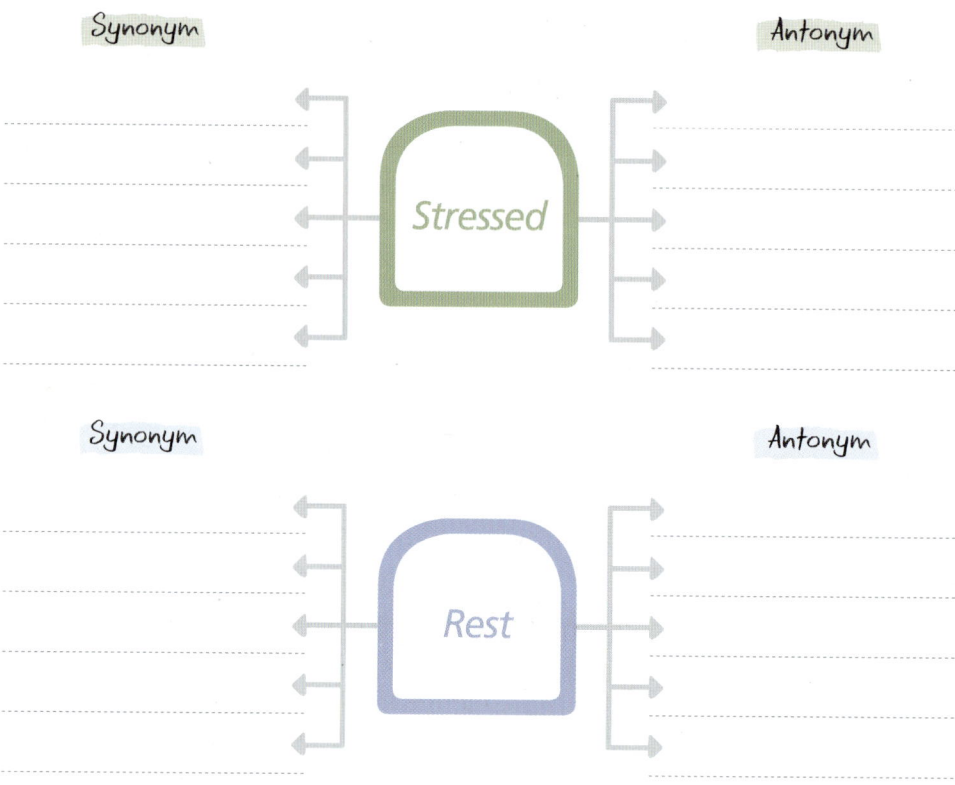

3 Sentence Building

Complete the sentences by filling in the blanks.
Refer to the grammar note above.

1. Where are you _____ this weekend?
2. I _____ reading a new book.
3. My team is _____ on a business trip to Moscow.
4. We _____ leaving right now.
5. They are _____ us at the train station.
6. You _____ talking too loudly.
7. I am _____ a play with my friend tonight.
8. What are _____ doing this weekend?

Grammar Note

Present continuous wh- questions

» What **are** you **doing** tonight?
» She/He **is playing** basketball.
» I **am watching** a movie.
» We/They **are waiting** for you.

» When **are** you **coming** here?
» I **am having** a party tonight.
» She/He **is sitting** in the living room.
» We **are playing** a game.

4. Dialogue Practice

Christopher	:	Are you doing anything tonight?
Jennifer	:	We were thinking of going to a movie.
Kathleen	:	Do you want to come along? I'm just booking the tickets right now.
Christopher	:	When are you going?
Jennifer	:	We're leaving at 7.
Christopher	:	I'm a little busy with work now, but I think I will finish soon.
Kathleen	:	Give us a call if you can come.
Jennifer	:	I really hope you can make it.
Christopher	:	Okay. Talk to you soon.

Comprehension Questions

1. Who is going to watch a movie?

1. What might the three people's relationship be?

1. What do you think the three people will do next?

5. Story Board

Look at the situation and complete the conversation.

Situation.01

What are you doing tonight? Are you busy?

Situation.02

What are you doing here? Are you going somewhere?

Lesson.07 What are you doing?

6 Comprehensive Listening

Listen to the dialogue and answer the questions.

A Circle True or False

- The two people had previously planned to go to dinner together.   True / False
- He is not going home now.   True / False
- The man will get his bag.   True / False
- The man and woman are married.   True / False

B Read each question and write full sentence responses.

- What do you think the relationship between the man and woman is?

- Where was the man going when they met?

- What will they do next?

- Where is the man now?

7 Speaking Patterns

Practice using the patterns below with a partner.

When are you…?
- When are you coming home?
- When are you leaving for vacation?
- When are you starting your new job?

I'm just…
- I'm just watching TV.
- I'm just eating dinner.
- I'm just waiting for a friend.

Are you…tonight?
- Are you coming to the party tonight?
- Are you working tonight?
- Are you eating out tonight?

Common Mistakes

What is correct? Read the sentences and circle the correct answer. Check the explanations at the back of the book.

01
You can set up your own bank account. / You can setup your own bank account.

02
The entire situation was a set up. / The entire situation was a setup.

03
She wanted to set up the television in the bedroom. / She wanted to setup the television in the bedroom.

8 Situational Use

What are some things you might say in each situation?

- Dinner time
- Visiting someone
- After work
- **What are you doing?**
- At home
- In the office
- At the shopping mall

Q: What other situations can you think of? Let's think and talk some more!

9 Fun Facts

Sagrada Família: Ongoing Architecture

The **Basílica i Temple Expiatori de la Sagrada Família (Basilica and Expiatory Church of the Holy Family)** is a Roman Catholic church in Barcelona, Spain, designed by Antoni Gaudí (1852–1926). It has been under construction since 1882, and is notable for combining Gothic and curvilinear Art Nouveau forms. However, it is still incomplete! Construction was interrupted by the Spanish Civil War and was resumed in the 1950s. Sagrada Família's construction has been progressing slowly, as it relies on private donations. Construction passed the midpoint in 2010 along with some of the project's greatest remaining challenges, and completion is expected in 2026.

Question

1. Did you already know about Sagrada Família? After reading the article, what do you know about it?

2. Discuss your opinions on this project. What do you think about the prolonged work?

3. Have you had an experience of dealing with long-term projects before? How was it? Provide pros and cons.

Review and Sneak Peek

Calling

_____
_____
_____
_____

Sneak Peek

01.
What time of day do you like? Why?

02.
Do you have any special plans for tonight? Explain.

Lesson 08 | Let me check my schedule

Learning Objectives: *After studying this lesson, you should be able to …*
- ☑ describe daily routines
- ☑ use the present continuous and simple present tenses to tell people about your current routine

1 Getting Started

A | Look at the picture and describe what you can see.

Practice the tongue twister with your partner. Who can say it faster?

» She saw Sheriff's shoes on the sofa. But was she so sure she saw Sheriff's shoes on the sofa?

B | Read the questions below and discuss with your partner.

1. What is your daily schedule like?
2. What is your ideal lifestyle? Do you prefer a fast, busy schedule or a slow, relaxed schedule?

2 Vocatree

Look at the words given below and brainstorm the synonyms and antonyms for the words.

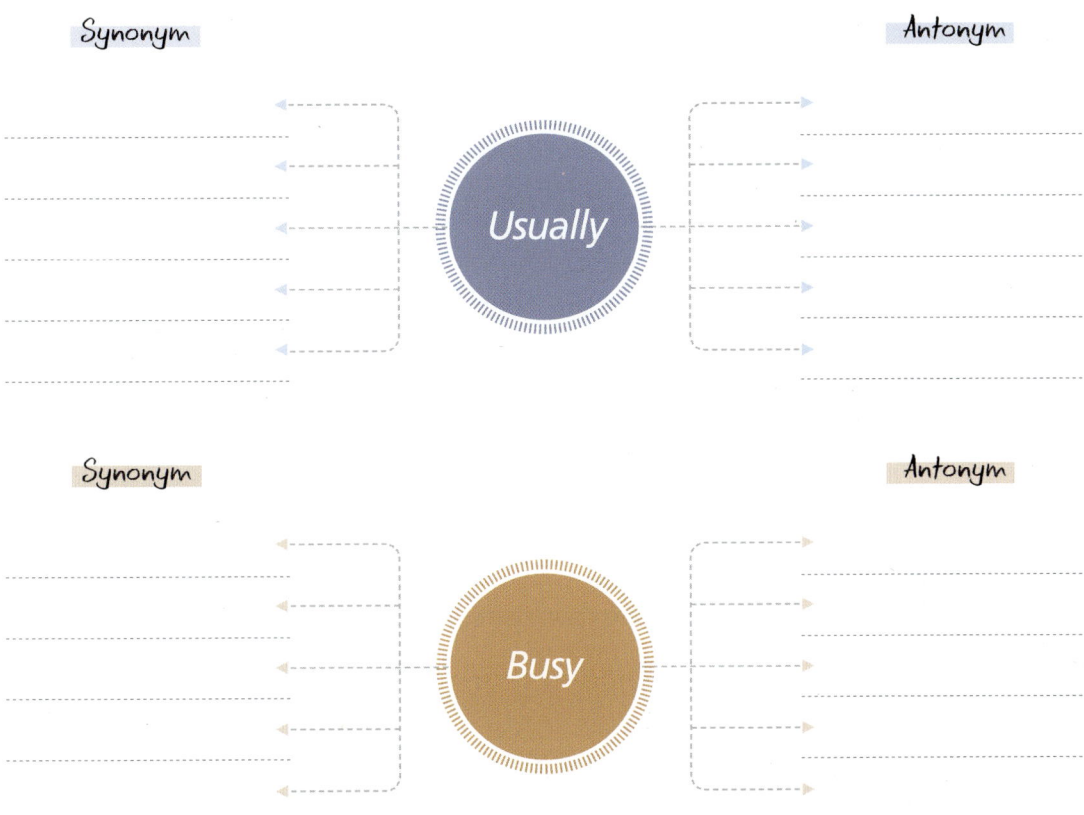

3 Sentence Building

Complete the sentences by filling in the blanks.
Refer to the grammar note above.

1. I usually _____ the subway to school.
2. She is _____ dinner at 7 o'clock today.
3. My brother always _____ home during his vacation.
4. My friend and I _____ lunch together every Tuesday.
5. I am _____ a class about art.
6. We are _____ to the museum this afternoon.
7. My mother always _____ breakfast for me.
8. I am _____ to the office today.

Grammar Note

Present Continuous and Simple Present for Daily Routines

» I **am taking** a cooking class.
» I **ride** the bus every day.
» We are **eating** lunch together at 12:30.
» He/She always **exercises** before work.
» I **visit** home every Christmas.

» I **am meeting** her after lunch.
» I **walk** my dog in the morning.
» We **clean** our house every Saturday.
» I **am leaving** before 10.
» She always **calls** me after work.

4 Dialogue Practice

Robert : Hey, Stan! It's been a long time!

Stan : What are you doing here at the park?

Robert : I often take a walk here during my lunch break.

Stan : How have you been lately?

Robert : I've been pretty busy with work. What are you doing this weekend?

Stan : We are planning to go camping this weekend.

Robert : Do you want to plan to get dinner sometime? I always eat near here after work.

Stan : That sounds good. Give me a call.

Comprehension Questions

1. Why is Robert at the park?
2. What do you think the two men's relationship is?
3. What might they do next?

5 Story Board

Look at the situation and complete the conversation.

Situation.01

What are you two doing this weekend? I'm thinking of having a party.

Situation.02

Where are you going now? Do you want to have dinner?

6 Comprehensive Listening

Listen to the dialogue and answer the questions.

A. Circle True or False

- The man and woman are co-workers.   True / False
- The woman will attend Johnny's party.   True / False
- They made plans for next week.   True / False
- They are members of the same gym.   True / False

B. Read each question and write full sentence responses.

- Where did the two people meet?

- What is Johnny doing this weekend?

- Why haven't the two people seen each other at the gym before?

- When will they probably meet again?

---

7 Speaking Patterns

Practice using the patterns below with a partner.

I always…after work.

- I always go to the gym after work.
- I always go shopping after work.
- I always check my e-mail after work.

We are planning to…this weekend.

- We are planning to meet this weekend.
- We are planning to visit the museum this weekend.
- We are planning to go to the movies this weekend.

I often…during my lunch break.

- I often call my wife during my lunch break.
- I often meet a friend during my lunch break.
- I often go to the bank during my lunch break.

Common Mistakes

**What is correct?
Read the sentences and circle the correct answer.
Check the explanations at the back of the book.**

01.
They're ready to go home.
/ Their ready to go home.

02.
Their is no one in the library.
/ There is no one in the library.

03.
There office is near the police station.
/ Their office is near the police station.

8 Situational Use

What are some things you might say in each situation?

- Arranging for a delivery
- Making a doctor's appointment
- Checking a friend's schedule
- Discussing Schedules
- Scheduling a meeting
- Making conversation
- Talking to your mother

Q: What other situations can you think of? Let's think and talk some more!

9 Fun Facts

Daily Activity Statistics

Source: US Bureau of Labor Statistics (June 22, 2023)

Activity	Average Hours / Day	Men	Women
Personal Care Activities	9.79	9.55	10.02
Sleeping	9.03	8.91	9.14
Eating and drinking	1.28	1.30	1.26
Household Activities	2.43	2.15	2.65
Housework	1.63	1.40	1.73
Food preparation and cleanup	1.07	0.83	1.23
Lawn and garden care	2.01	2.34	1.58
Household management	0.84	0.88	0.81
Purchasing goods and services	1.70	1.65	1.74
Consumer goods purchases	0.89	0.83	0.93
Professional and personal care services	1.23	1.35	1.16
Caring for and helping household members	2.21	1.83	2.44
Caring for and helping household children	1.99	1.67	2.19
Caring for and helping non-household members	2.01	1.92	2.06
Caring for and helping non-household adults	1.11	1.13	1.10

Activity	Average Hours / Day	Men	Women
Working and Work-related Activities	8.01	8.29	7.66
Working	7.66	7.91	7.35
Educational activities	5.46	5.15	5.75
Attending class	4.93	4.54	5.31
Homework and research	2.88	2.83	2.93
Organizational, civic, and religious activities	2.20	2.42	2.05
Religious and spiritual activities	1.54	1.58	1.51
Volunteering (organizational and civic activities)	2.26	2.63	2.04
Leisure and Sports	5.47	5.82	5.14
Socializing and communicating	1.95	1.90	1.99
Watching television	3.65	3.90	3.40
Participating in sports, exercise, and recreation	1.44	1.55	1.31
Telephone calls, mail, and e-mail	0.89	0.82	0.95
Other activities, not elsewhere classified	1.30	1.34	1.27

Question

1. Do any activities take more or less time than you expected? Which surprise you, and why?
2. Write down your daily schedule. How much time do you spend on each activity? Compare your schedule with the data above.
3. Discuss how you manage your schedule and time. Do you have any strategies? Is there anything you would like to change?

Review and Sneak Peek

Calling
_____
_____

Sneak Peek

01. What occupations can you name? What is your current job?
02. What is your dream job? Explain.

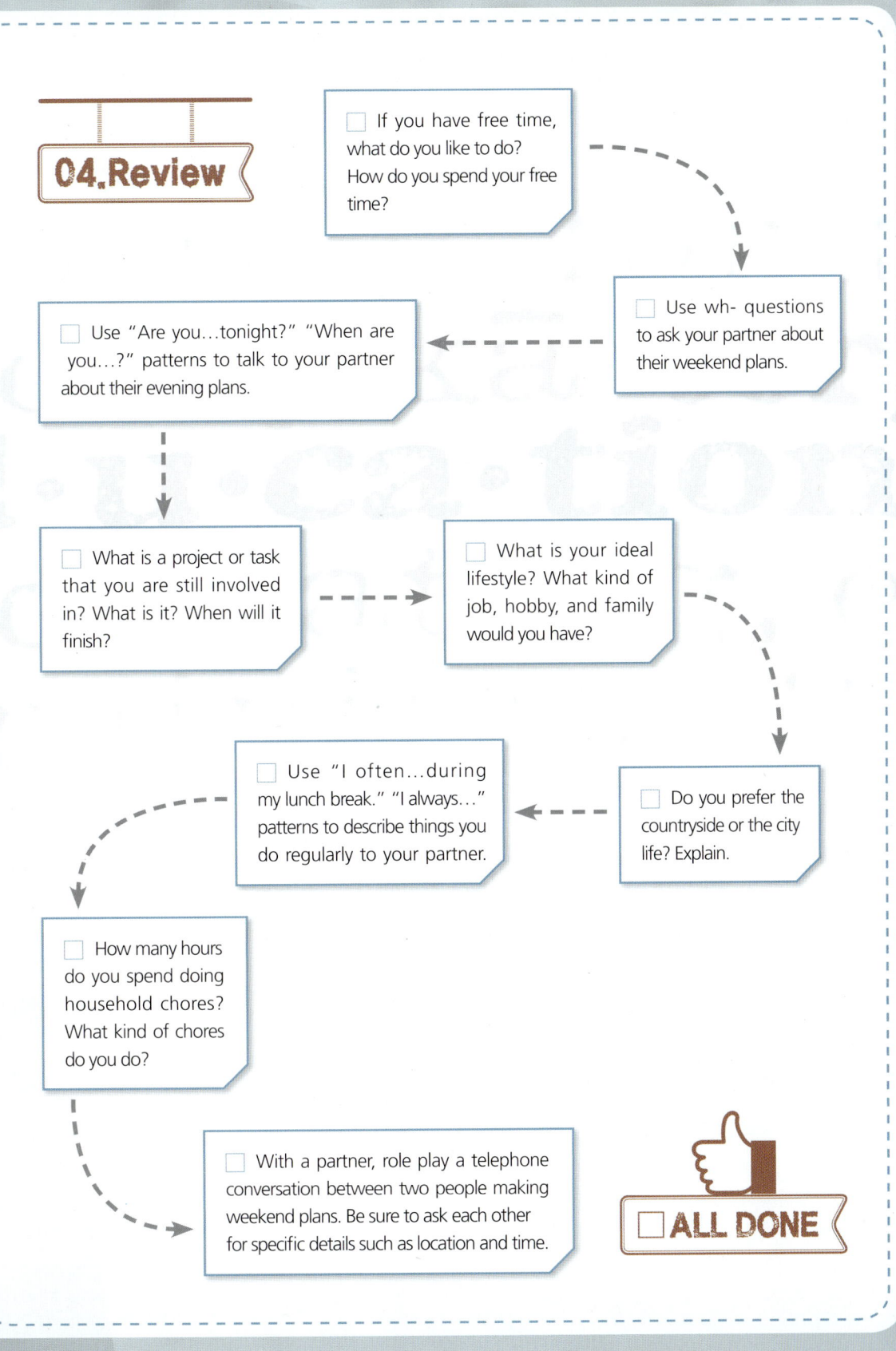

Lesson 09 Going to work

Learning Objectives : *After studying this lesson, you should be able to …*
- ☑ talk about occupations
- ☑ use simple present tense wh- questions to ask others about their work

1 Getting Started

A | Look at the picture and describe what you can see.

B | Read the questions below and discuss with your partner.

❶ What do you think is an ideal occupation? Why?

❷ Describe the place where you work or have worked. What did you like and dislike about it?

Tongue Twisters

Practice the tongue twister with your partner. Who can say it faster?

» I thought a thought, but the thought I thought wasn't the thought I thought I thought.

2 Vocatree

Look at the words given below, brainstorm the synonyms and antonyms for the words.

[Synonym]   [Antonym]

Challenging

[Synonym]   [Antonym]

Interesting

3 Sentence Building

**Complete the sentences by filling in the blanks.
Refer to the grammar note on the right.**

1. When _____ your team usually take vacation?

2. What department do _____ work in?

3. Where _____ your manager sit?

4. _____ do you get to leave work?

5. _____ do you usually sit?

6. What _____ do you eat lunch?

7. _____ does your wife do?

8. When do _____ get to take a break?

Grammar Note

Simple present tense wh- questions with "do"

» What **do** you **do**?
» Where **do** you **work**?
» When **do** you start **work**?
» What **does** he/she **do**?
» What time **do** you **leave** the office?

» What **do** you **do** after work?
» What time **does** your team **finish** work?
» What **does** your company **produce**?
» Where **do** you usually **eat** lunch?
» What **do** you **do** at the office?

Lesson.09 Going to work | 55

4 Dialogue Practice

David	: It's great seeing you again. What do you do now?
Susie	: I work as a receptionist, but I don't like it much. In the future, I'd like to do what my husband does.
David	: What does he do?
Susie	: He works as an accountant.
David	: Isn't it a difficult job?
Susie	: Yes, but his work seems interesting. My current job is not challenging enough.
David	: I can understand that. My job is a little boring at times.
Susie	: Really? What do you do?

Comprehension Questions

1. What does Susie do?
2. How might David and Susie know each other?
3. What might they talk about next?

5 Story Board

Look at the situation and complete the conversation.

Situation.01

I haven't seen you in forever! I heard you changed jobs. What do you do now?

Situation.02

I work as a tutor now, but I'm thinking of changing my job.

6 Comprehensive Listening

Listen to the dialogue and answer the questions.

A Circle True or False

- The two went to school together.   True / False
- The woman works for her father.   True / False
- The man wants to run a chain of shoe stores.   True / False
- The man is unhappy with his job.   True / False

B Read the following questions and write full sentence responses.

- Where does the woman work?

- What is their relationship?

- What does the man's father do?

- Why might he want to change jobs?

7 Speaking Patterns

Practice using the patterns below with a partner.

I work as a (an)....
- » I work as a nurse.
- » I work as a mechanic.
- » I work as a tutor.

In the future, I'd like to....
- » In the future, I'd like to go back to school.
- » In the future, I'd like to start my own business.
- » In the future, I'd like to write a book.

What does...do?
- » What does your wife do?
- » What does Bill do?
- » What does your father do?

Common Mistakes

What is correct?
Read the sentences and circle the correct answer.
Check the explanations at the back of the book.

01. ....
This book is good. / This book is well

02. ....
You speak English good. / You speak English well.

03. ....
Did the movie do good at the box office? / Did the movie do well at the box office?

Lesson.09 Going to work

8 Situational Use

What are some things you might say in each situation?

Q: What other situations can you think of? Let's think and talk some more!

9 Fun Facts

Unusual Jobs That Pay Well

When people think about high-paying jobs, they usually think of doctors, lawyers, and CEOs. However, some unexpected jobs also pay a decent income. The following is a list of 15 unusual jobs that pay surprisingly well:

- **Bereavement coordinator** $69,960 per year
- **Art therapist** $70,182 per year
- **Childbirth educator** $70,415 per year
- **Genetic counselor** $72,582 per year
- **Bingo or casino manager** $73,959 per year
- **Recreation therapist** $75,196 per year
- **Orthotist and prosthetist** $80,947 per year
- **Fire investigator** $86,218 per year
- **Voice-over artist** $92,194 per year
- **Elevator mechanic** $99,000 per year
- **Respiratory therapist** $105,908 per year
- **Ethical hacker** $109,720 per year
- **Toy designer** $114,845 per year
- **Periodontist** $229,797 per year
- **Podiatrist** $247,741 per year

Question

1. Why might some of these positions pay so well?
2. How important is income to you when choosing a job? Why?
3. What are some high-paying jobs in your country?

Calling
_____
_____
_____
_____

Sneak Peek

01.
What are you doing this weekend? Do you have any special plans?

02.
What do you usually do during your free time? Explain.

Lesson 10: Weekend plans

Learning Objectives: *After studying this lesson, you should be able to …*
- ☑ discuss future plans in detail
- ☑ use "be going to" and "will" to inform others about your plans

1 Getting Started

A | **Look at the picture and describe what you can see.**

Practice the tongue twister with your partner. Who can say it faster?

» I wish to wish the wish you wish to wish, but if you wish the wish the witch wishes, I won't wish the wish you wish to wish.

B | **Read the questions below and discuss with your partner.**

1. Are you good at making plans? Why or why not?
2. In what situations is it important to make plans?

2 Vocatree

Look at the words given below, brainstorm the synonyms and antonyms for the words.

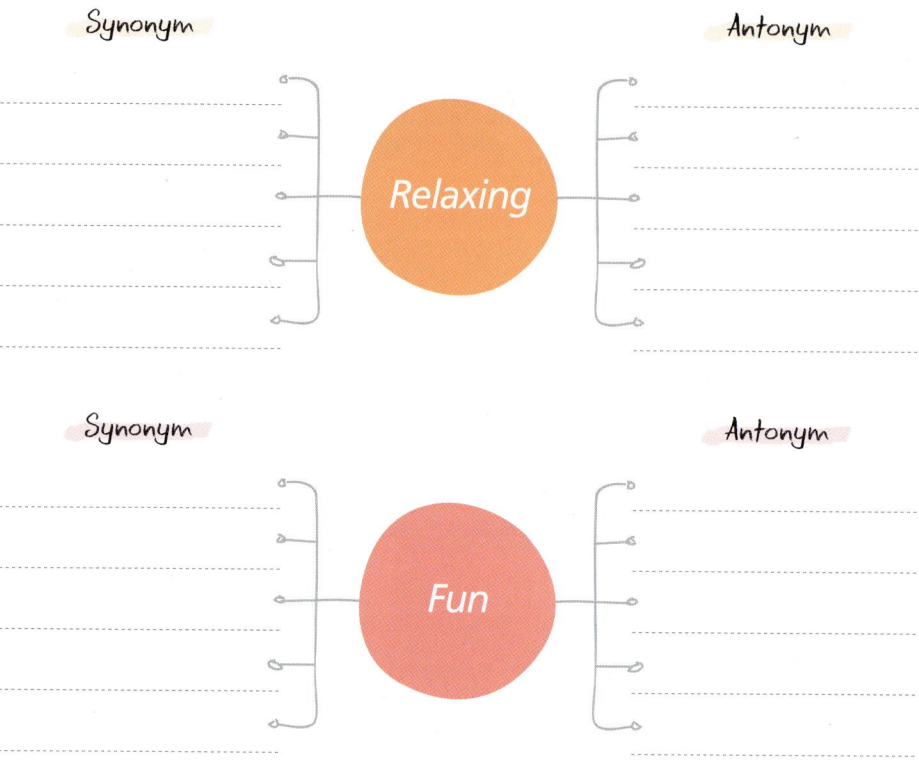

3 Sentence Building

Complete the sentences by filling in the blanks. Refer to the grammar note on the right.

1. I _____ call you and make an appointment.
2. She is _____ to leave for vacation tomorrow.
3. My brother _____ pick up the package.
4. I am going to _____ a movie tonight.
5. I will _____ the ingredients today.
6. My co-workers _____ to eat together tonight.
7. We will _____ the bus home tonight.
8. I _____ arrange an appointment later.

Grammar Note

Future tense with "be going to" and "will"

» He/She **will** call you later.
» I **will** bring you some coffee.
» I **will** check my schedule and let you know.
» You **will** transfer the money to me.
» She **will** let you know the schedule later.

» I **am going to** visit my friend for vacation.
» She/He **is going to** meet us at the restaurant.
» We **are going to** travel around Europe this summer.
» My mother **is going to** cook dinner at Christmas.
» I **am going to** have a party tonight.

4 Dialogue Practice

Margaret : What are your plans for the weekend?

Eric : This weekend, I'm going to a jazz music festival.

Margaret : That sounds like so much fun! Where is it?

Eric : It's going to be held at Olympic Park. Do you want to go?

Margaret : I think I have to work on Saturday, but I'm not sure yet.

Eric : It would be great if you could make it.

Margaret : Tonight, I will check my schedule and let you know.

Eric : Okay. Let me know. If you can go, I will get a ticket for you.

Comprehension Questions

1. What are Eric's plans?
2. What might Margaret be doing this weekend?
3. What do you think they will talk about next?

5 Story Board

Look at the situation and complete the conversation.

Situation.01

What are you two doing this weekend?

Situation.02

What do we need to do before our vacation?

6. Comprehensive Listening

Listen to the dialogue and answer the questions.

A Circle True or False

- They are co-workers.   True / False
- The woman will find the man's bag.   True / False
- The man will come home at lunchtime.   True / False
- The woman will watch the soccer game.   True / False

B Read the following questions and write full sentence responses.

- What will the man do tomorrow?

- What will the woman do tonight?

- Where will the man eat lunch?

- What might their relationship be?

7. Speaking Patterns

Practice using the patterns below with a partner.

This weekend, I'm going to....

- This weekend, I'm going to meet a friend.
- This weekend, I'm going to ride my bike.
- This weekend, I'm going to be out of town.

I will…for you.

- I will find that book for you.
- I will make an appointment for you.
- I will cook dinner for you.

Tonight, I will….

- Tonight, I will clean the house.
- Tonight, I will go to the grocery store.
- Tonight, I will go to bed early.

Common Mistakes

What is correct?
Read the sentences and circle the correct answer.
Check the explanations at the back of the book.

01
The book has lost many of its pages.
/ The book has lost many of it's pages.

02
Its not cold enough to wear a coat.
/ It's not cold enough to wear a coat.

03
She told me that its time for bed.
/ She told me that it's time for bed.

8 Situational Use

What are some things you might say in each situation?

9 Fun Facts

If you haven't heard about the term "bucket list," it is a list of all the goals you want to achieve, dreams you want to fulfill, and life experiences you desire to have before you die.

Popular Bucket List Ideas :

- [ ] Travel around the world
- [ ] Learn a new language
- [ ] Try a profession in a different field
- [ ] Achieve your ideal weight
- [ ] Run a marathon
- [ ] Take part in a triathlon
- [ ] Take up a new sport
- [ ] Go scuba diving or snorkeling
- [ ] Give a heartfelt surprise to someone
- [ ] Fly in a hot-air balloon

Question

❶ From the list given, choose one thing you would wish to try. Why did you choose it?

❷ How do you maintain a balance between what you have to do and what you want to do?

❸ Make your own bucket list with at least five things. What steps can you take to achieve them?

Review and Sneak Peek

Calling

_____
_____
_____
_____

Sneak Peek

01.
Do you have any hobbies? What are they?

02.
What are some popular hobbies in your country?

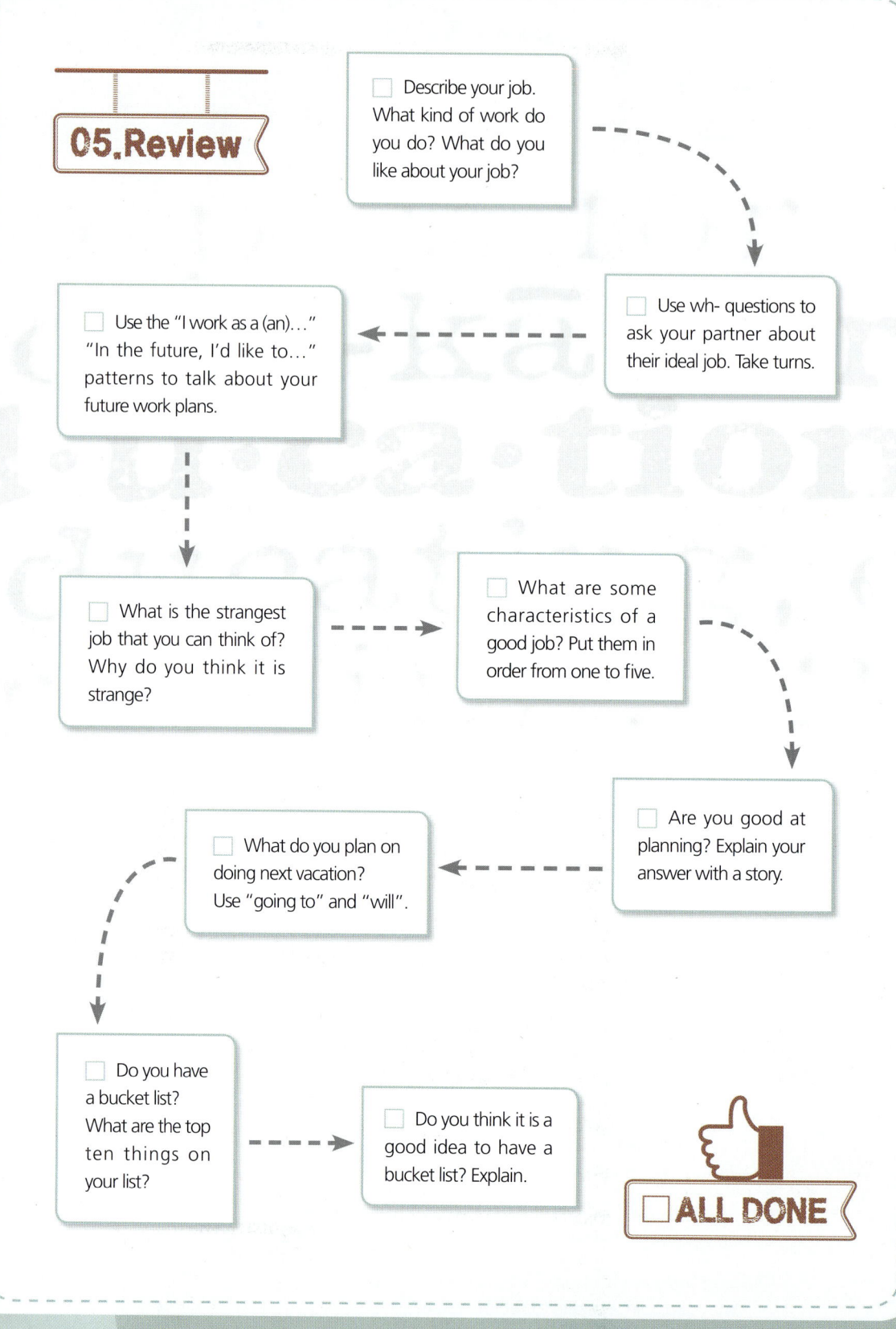

Lesson 11

These are my hobbies

Learning Objectives : *After studying this lesson, you should be able to …*

- ☑ discuss your hobbies in detail
- ☑ use gerunds to describe your favorite activities

1 Getting Started

A | **Look at the picture and describe what you can see.**

Practice the tongue twister with your partner. Who can say it faster?

» Fuzzy Wuzzy was a bear.
Fuzzy Wuzzy had no hair.
Fuzzy Wuzzy wasn't very fuzzy, was he?

B | **Read the questions below and discuss with your partner.**

1. Do you have any hobbies? What are they?
2. What do you think are the benefits of participating in recreational activities?

2 Vocatree

Look at the words given below, brainstorm the synonyms and antonyms for the words.

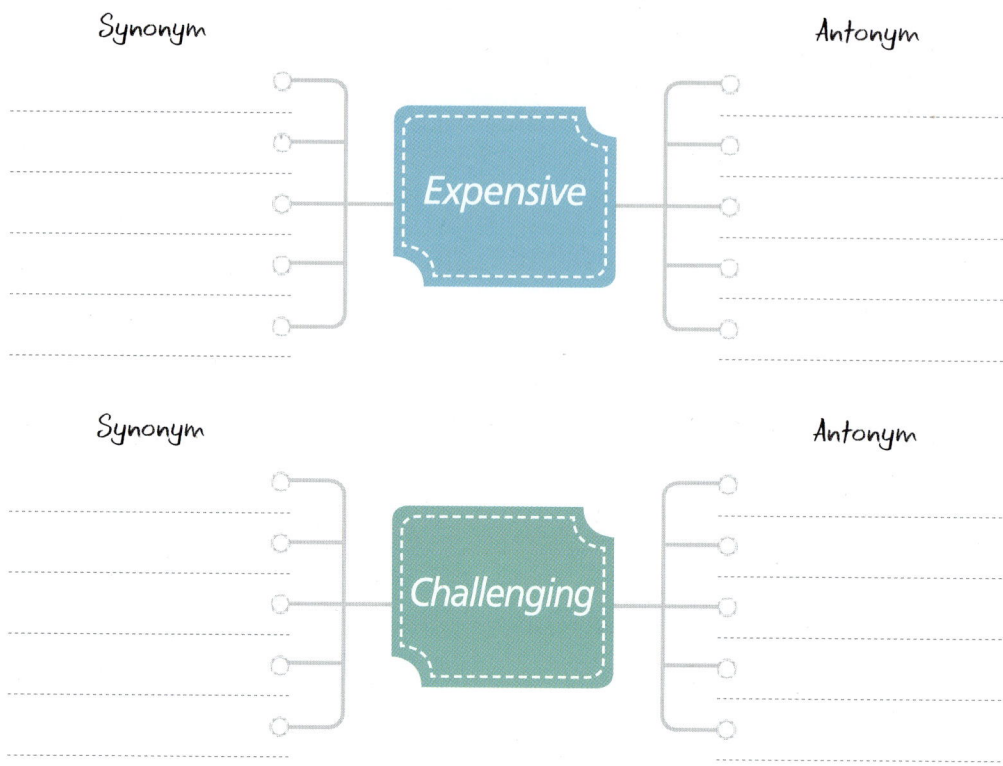

3 Sentence Building

Complete the sentences by filling in the blanks. Refer to the grammar note on the right.

1. I enjoy _____ (ski) in the winter.

2. Do you like _____ (ride) horses?

3. She loves _____ new foods.

4. I have always _____ going camping.

5. My father _____ watching musicals.

6. I enjoy _____ new museum exhibits.

7. What kinds of movies do you _____ watching?

8. I tried _____ last weekend.

Grammar Note

Gerunds -ing form

» I enjoy **learning** new languages.
» We both enjoy **reading**.
» I like **watching** action movies.
» I have always liked **playing** soccer.
» Do you like **trying** new restaurants?

» Do you enjoy **riding** bicycles?
» I like **cooking** for my friends.
» He/She loves **traveling** abroad.
» I tried **scuba diving** last summer.
» I want to try **snowboarding**.

4 Dialogue Practice

Amanda	:	Do you have any hobbies?
Jason	:	I enjoy horseback riding in my free time. Have you ever tried it?
Amanda	:	I tried it on my last vacation, but I didn't like it much.
Jason	:	Oh no, why?
Amanda	:	Honestly, I was a little scared of being on such a big animal. It was my first time.
Jason	:	You probably just need more practice. I find horseback riding a lot of fun.
Amanda	:	Maybe I could go with you sometime.
Jason	:	That would be fun.

Comprehension Questions

1. What are they discussing?
2. Why was Amanda scared?
3. What other activities could Jason recommend for Amanda?

5 Story Board

Look at the situation and complete the conversation.

Situation.01

How was your vacation? Did you try any water sports at the resort?

Situation.02

What do you usually do on the weekends?

6 Comprehensive Listening

Listen to the dialogue and answer the questions.

A | Circle True or False

- The woman likes to go camping. (*True* / *False*)
- The man is a good fisherman. (*True* / *False*)
- They will go camping next weekend. (*True* / *False*)
- The woman likes rainbow trout. (*True* / *False*)

B | Read the following questions and write full sentence responses.

- What does the man enjoy?

- What does the man do when he camps?

- What will the man bring the woman?

- Do you think they know each other well? Why or why not?

7 Speaking Patterns

Practice using the patterns below with a partner.

Have you ever tried…?
- » Have you ever tried eating Indian food?
- » Have you ever tried wind surfing?
- » Have you ever tried knitting?

I enjoy…in my free time.
- » I enjoy cooking new foods in my free time.
- » I enjoy doing yoga in my free time.
- » I enjoy painting in my free time.

I find….
- » I find skydiving very exciting.
- » I find Mexican food to be too spicy.
- » I find reading to be boring.

Common Mistakes

What is correct?
Read the sentences and circle the correct answer.
Check the explanations at the back of the book.

---01
Lisa is the girl with who I'm driving to the beach.
/ Lisa is the girl with whom I'm driving to the beach.

---02
Jack is the one who wants to eat pizza.
/ Jack is the one whom wants to eat pizza.

---03
This is the doctor who I told you about.
/ This is the doctor whom I told you about.

8 Situational Use

What are some things you might say in each situation?

- With a new friend
- At dinner
- Making conversation
- Talking at lunch
- Discussing weekend plans
- On a blind date

Q: What other situations can you think of? Let's think and talk some more!

9 Fun Facts

50 Most Popular Hobbies

01. Reading	14. Team sports	27. Bicycling	40. Animal care
02. Watching TV	15. Shopping	28. Playing cards	41. Bowling
03. Family time	16. Traveling	29. Hiking	42. Painting
04. Going to the movies	17. Sleeping	30. Cooking	43. Running
05. Fishing	18. Socializing	31. Eating out	44. Dancing
06. Computer	19. Sewing	32. Dating online	45. Horseback riding
07. Gardening	20. Golf	33. Swimming	46. Tennis
08. Renting movies	21. Church activities	34. Camping	47. Theater
09. Walking	22. Relaxing	35. Skiing	48. Billiards
10. Exercise	23. Playing music	36. Working on cars	49. Beach
11. Listening to music	24. Housework	37. Writing	50. Volunteer work
12. Entertaining	25. Crafts	38. Boating	
13. Hunting	26. Watching sports	39. Motorcycling	

Question

1. Look at the list of hobbies above.
   Are there any hobbies that you already do on the list? Can you add any more?

2. Do you normally have time for hobbies on the weekend?
   Discuss the advantages and disadvantages of having hobbies.

3. What hobbies do you want to have in the future?
   Why don't you or can't you do it now? Why do you want to do it?

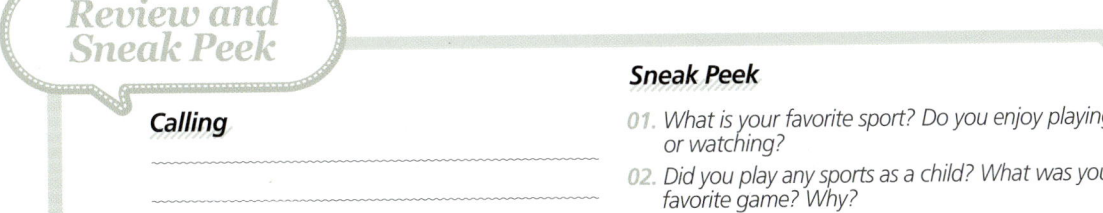

Review and Sneak Peek

Calling

_____

Sneak Peek

01. What is your favorite sport? Do you enjoy playing or watching?
02. Did you play any sports as a child? What was your favorite game? Why?

Lesson 12
I've been playing for a while

Learning Objectives : *After studying this lesson, you should be able to …*
- ☑ talk about your favorite hobbies and sports
- ☑ describe the length of time you have done activities using the present perfect tense

1 Getting Started

A | Look at the picture and describe what you can see.

Tongue Twisters

Practice the tongue twister with your partner. Who can say it faster?

» One-one was a race horse.
Two-two was one, too.
One-one won one race.
Two-two won one, too.

B | Read the questions below and discuss with your partner.

1. Have you ever been to a live sports event? What was it like?
2. What was your favorite sport as a child? Has that changed?

2 Vocatree

Look at the words given below and brainstorm the synonyms and antonyms for the words.

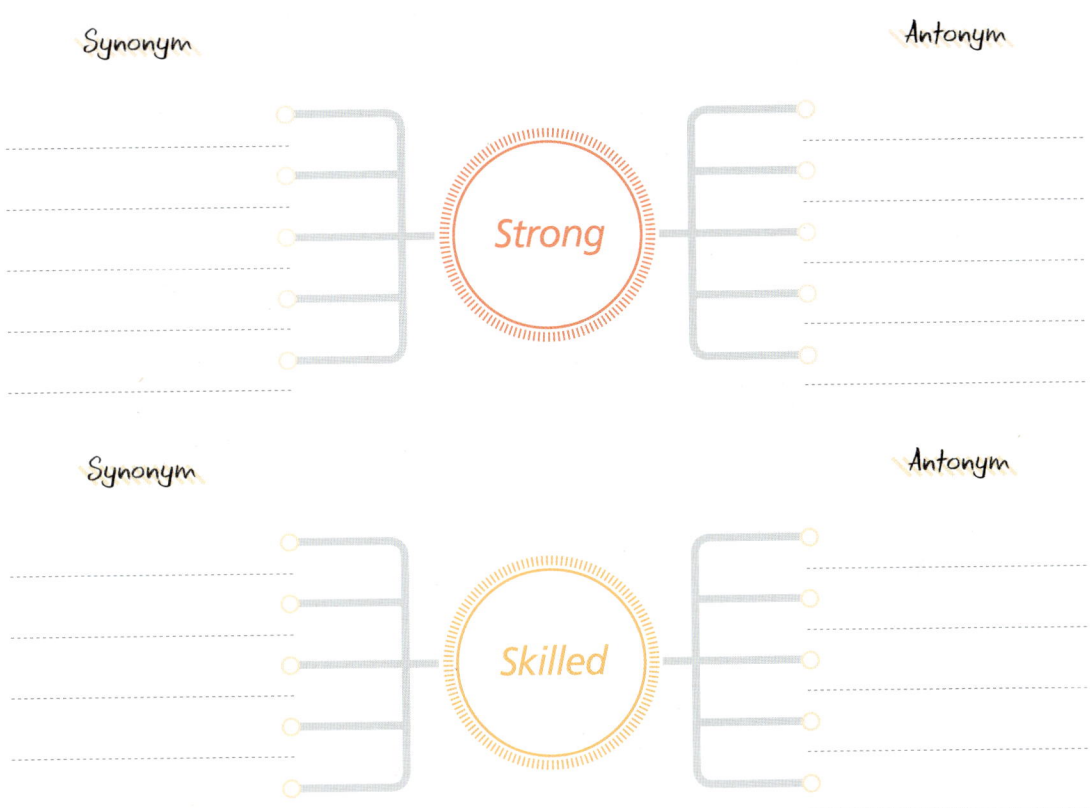

3 Sentence Building

Complete the sentences by filling in the blanks. Refer to the grammar note on the right.

1. I have played tennis _____ 12 years.
2. My sister has _____ piano since she was 10.
3. I have _____ bikes since I was 7.
4. We _____ played volleyball together for 5 years.
5. My family has skied together every winter vacation _____ 1998.
6. You _____ played football since you were 12.
7. Our club _____ met every Saturday for 2 years.
8. My mother has _____ yoga for more than 20 years.

Grammar Note

Using present perfect tense with "for" and "since"

» I **have played** football for 5 years.
» She **has practiced** flute since she was 7.
» I **have done** yoga for 5 years.
» We **have played** soccer together since 2006.
» I **have ridden** horses since I was 9.

» She/He **has studied** French for 10 years.
» I **have played** basketball since I was 12.
» They **have skied** together for years.
» You **have run** marathons since you were 20.
» I **have practiced** badminton since I was 15.

4 Dialogue Practice

Mrs. Bell	: I can't believe how well you and your brother play!
Rosie	: Thank you. I'm glad you liked the song.
Mrs. Bell	: How long have you been learning?
Rosie	: I've been playing the piano since I was 12 years old … and my brother has been playing guitar for almost 15 years.
Bob	: It hasn't been that long, has it? I've been playing since I was 12.
Rosie	: And you're 27 now, so 15 years.
Bob	: I guess my sister is right. It doesn't feel like it's been that long.
Mrs. Bell	: Anyway, you're both very talented musicians. Could you play me another song?

Comprehension Questions

1. What instrument does Rosie play?
2. What did Rosie and Bob do before the conversation?
3. What might they do next?

5 Story Board

Look at the situation and complete the conversation.

Situation.01

That was great! How long have you been playing?

Situation.02

Your brother is great! He must have played for a long time.

6. Comprehensive Listening

Listen to the dialogue and answer the questions.

A. Circle True or False

- The man plays in a band.   True / False
- The woman played for the man.   True / False
- The man brought his flute.   True / False
- The woman enjoys playing the cello.   True / False

B. Read each question and write full sentence responses.

- When did she start playing the flute?

- Who just played a song?

- When did the man learn the cello?

- What might the man do next?

7. Speaking Patterns

Practice using the patterns below with a partner.

I have…since I was 12 years old.
- » I have skied since I was 12 years old.
- » I have surfed since I was 12 years old.
- » I have enjoyed running since I was 12 years old.

I have been playing….
- » I have been playing for 3 years.
- » I have been playing since I was 9.
- » I have been playing since 2008.

My brother has…for almost 15 years.
- » My brother has played football for almost 15 years.
- » My brother has studied French for almost 15 years.
- » My brother has participated in the club for almost 15 years.

Common Mistakes

What is correct?
Read the sentences and circle the correct answer.
Check the explanations at the back of the book.

01.
She was tired, to. / She was tired, too.

02.
There were two birds on the tree. / There were too birds on the tree.

03.
I want to visit the museum. / I want too visit the museum.

8 Situational Use

What are some things you might say in each situation?

Q: What other situations can you think of? Let's think and talk some more!

9 Fun Facts

10 Olympic Games Trivia

01. In the ancient Olympics, all athletes competed nude.

02. The only Olympic event in which mother and daughter competed together was the golf tournament of 1900.

03. The only Olympian awarded the Nobel Prize was Philip Noel-Baker of Great Britain. He won the silver in the 1500-meter run in 1920, and won the Nobel Peace prize in 1959 for his support of multilateral nuclear disarmament.

04. The first black athlete to compete at the Olympics was Constantin Henriquez de Zubiera of France in 1900.

05. At the first modern Olympics in Athens in 1896, silver medals were awarded to the winners and bronze to the second place.

06. No women competed in 1896, as de Coubertin felt that the inclusion would be "impractical, uninteresting, unaesthetic, and incorrect."

07. The oldest man to compete in the Summer Olympic Games was Oscar Swahn of Sweden in shooting. He became the oldest gold medalist when he won gold at 64 in 1912, and the oldest medalist when he won silver in 1920 at the age of 72.

08. The oldest woman to compete in the Olympics was British rider Lorna Johnstone, who participated in Equestrian in 1972 at the age of 70.

09. India has the lowest number of total Olympic medals per capita.

10. The record for the longest name for an Olympic champion is by female Thai weightlifter Prapawadee Jaroenrattanatarakoon. She won the gold medal in the 53 kilograms category at Beijing 2008. Her name was so long that it did not fit onto the scoreboard, which listed her as "J."

Question

① Talk about the Olympics. What types of sports are included? What is the spirit of the Olympics? When and where does it happen?

② Do you watch the Olympic Games? Discuss a memorable Olympic Games or some memorable athletes you have seen so far.

③ What is your favorite sport in the Olympics? Why?

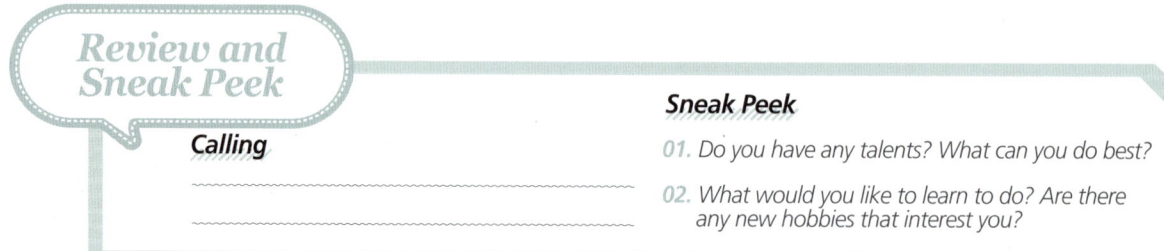

Review and Sneak Peek

Calling
_____
_____

Sneak Peek

01. Do you have any talents? What can you do best?

02. What would you like to learn to do? Are there any new hobbies that interest you?

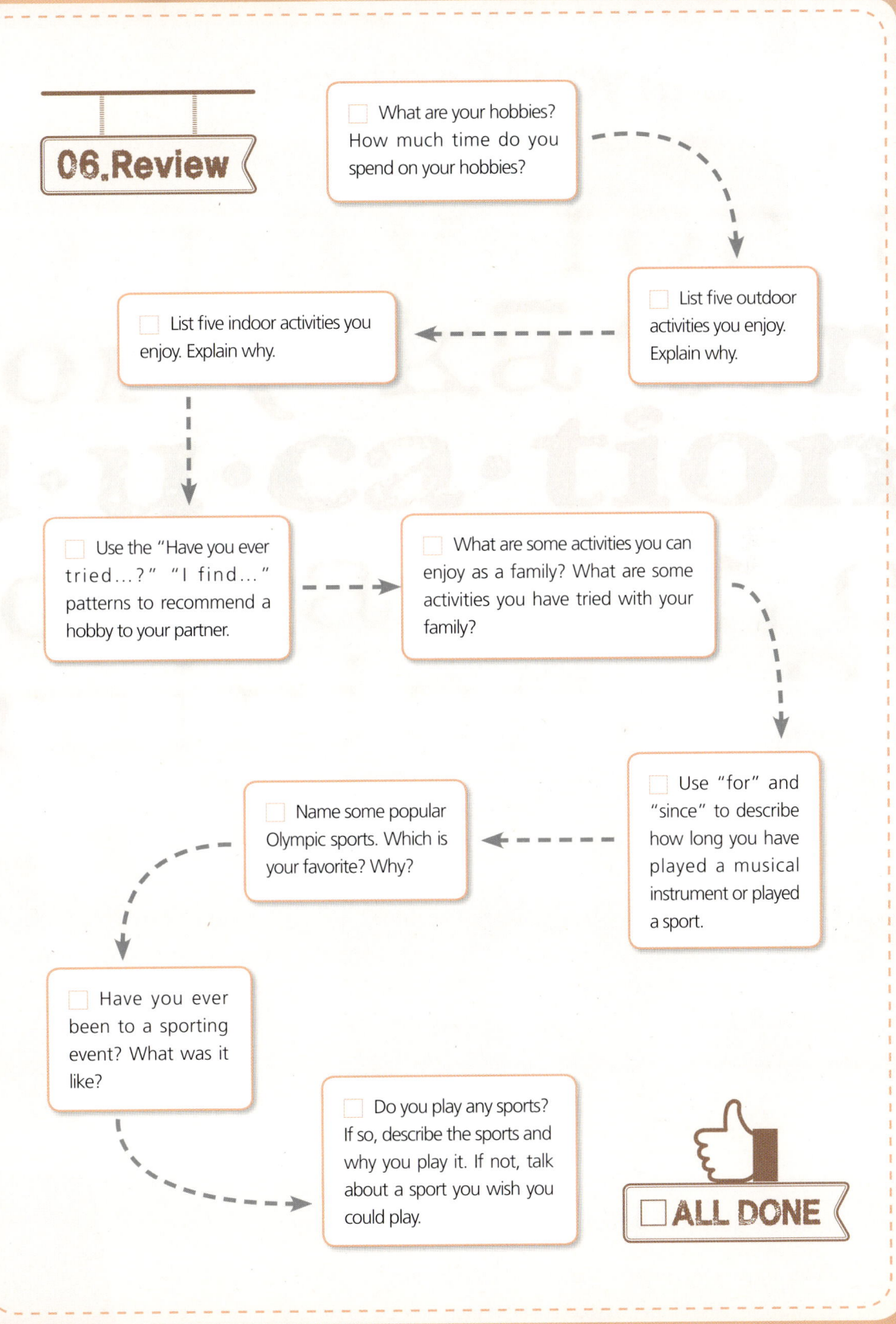

Lesson 13
Can you? Can't you?

Learning Objectives: *After studying this lesson, you should be able to …*
- ☑ talk about your abilities and talents
- ☑ use "can," "have to," and "able to" to describe your capabilities

1 Getting Started

A | **Look at the picture and describe what you can see.**

Practice the tongue twister with your partner. Who can say it faster?

» I saw Susie sitting in a shoe shine shop. Where she sits, she shines, and where she shines, she sits.

B | **Read the questions below and discuss with your partner.**

1. Do you have any special skills or talents? What are they?
2. What are some things that you have to do every day? Do you do any chores?

2 Vocatree

Look at the words given below and brainstorm the synonyms and antonyms for the words.

3 Sentence Building

Complete the sentences by filling in the blanks. Refer to the grammar note on the right.

1. My sister can _____ the flute well.
2. I am able to _____ a bike for 20 kilometers.
3. I can _____ my own clothes.
4. I _____ to read French.
5. My father _____ able to ski down black diamond runs.
6. I _____ to do taxes for work.
7. My friend can play _____ like a professional.
8. We have to _____ off the lights before we go home.

Grammar Note

"can" vs. "have to" vs. "able to" for talents and ability

» **I have to** cook dinner every night.
» **Can** you play any instruments?
» I'm **able to** parallel park.
» My brother **can** fly an airplane.
» He/She **has to** travel often for work.

» **I can** speak four languages.
» She is **able to** fix the sink.
» We **can** help you finish the project.
» **I can** run three miles.
» **I have to** help my boss with this paperwork.

4 Dialogue Practice

Dan : Are you ready to leave?

Grace : Not yet. Just a few more minutes.

Dan : What are you doing?

Grace : I have to reply to a few e-mails for work. I have to write in Spanish.

Dan : When will you be able to finish? We'll be late for the movie.

Grace : It shouldn't take long. I can write Spanish well.

Dan : Okay. I'll wait in the car.

Grace : I'll be ready soon. Don't worry.

Comprehension Questions

1. Where are they going?
2. How do you think Dan feels?
3. What kind of work do you think Grace might do?

5 Story Board

Look at the situation and complete the conversation.

Situation.01

If we hire you, when will you be able to start?

Situation.02

How did you get so good at this program? It's so hard for me.

6 Comprehensive Listening

Listen to the dialogue and answer the questions.

A Circle True or False

- The man will help her next weekend.   True / False
- The woman is good at cooking.   True / False
- The man understands the computer program.   True / False
- The man is busy now.   True / False

B Read each question and write full sentence responses.

- What does the woman need help with?
  _____

- Why can't the man help her today?
  _____

- What does the woman offer to do for him?
  _____

- Why is the man good at the program?
  _____

7 Speaking Patterns

Practice using the patterns below with a partner.

I have to…for work.
- I have to do a lot of paperwork for work.
- I have to finish this project for work.
- I have to answer e-mails for work.

I can…well.
- I can speak Chinese well.
- I can drive a manual well.
- I can use the new computer program well.

When will you be able to…?
- When will you be able to call me back?
- When will you be able to finish this project?
- When will you be able to meet me?

Common Mistakes

What is correct?
Read the sentences and circle the correct answer.
Check the explanations at the back of the book.

01
He went into the army. / He went in to the army.

02
The girl dived back into rescue the drowning boy. / The girl dived back in to rescue the drowning boy.

03
The council is looking into the scandal. / The council is looking in to the scandal.

Lesson.13 Can you? Can't you? | 79

8 Situational Use
What are some things you might say in each situation?

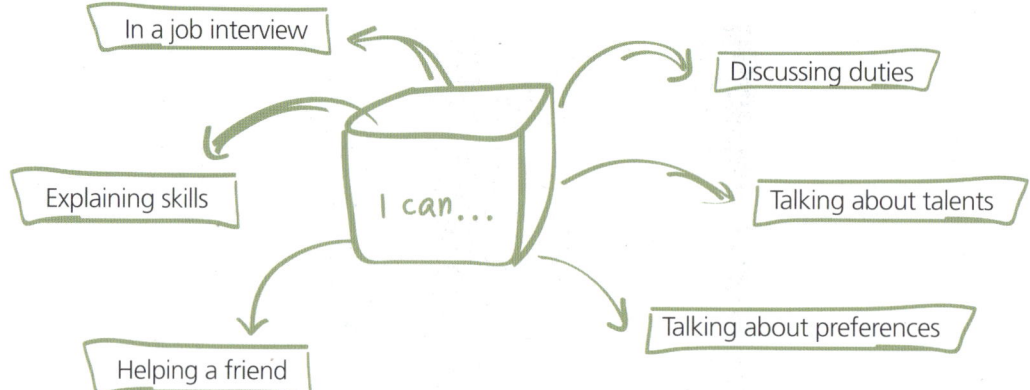

9 Fun Facts
Supernatural Abilities

01. Teleportation	**11.** Mind Reading
02. Healing Ability	**12.** Super Strength
03. Time Manipulation	**13.** Super Speed
04. Mind Control	**14.** Talking to Animals
05. Shapeshifting	**15.** Fast Reflexes
06. Invincibility	**16.** Underwater Breathing
07. Super Intelligence	**17.** Walking through Walls
08. Time Travel	**18.** Weather Control
09. Invisibility	**19.** Night Vision
10. Flight	**20.** Flexibility

Question

❶ Think about and describe a superhero with one of the super powers listed. Where did you see the person, and how does he or she use the super power?

❷ List the three super powers you wish to have. Why would you like to have them, and why is it in that order?

❸ If you could give a super power to the people you know, what would you give them? Why?

Review and Sneak Peek

Calling
_____
_____
_____
_____

Sneak Peek

01.
How often do you make plans with friends? What do you usually do?

02.
How can you politely decline an invitation? Explain.

Lesson 14: Would you like to...?

Learning Objectives: *After studying this lesson, you should be able to ...*
- ☑ invite someone to do something
- ☑ use verbs to politely make, accept, and decline invitations

1 Getting Started

A | Look at the picture and describe what you can see.

B | Read the questions below and discuss with your partner.

1. When was the last time you invited someone to do something? What was it?
2. What are some ways that you could decline an invitation?

Tongue Twisters

Practice the tongue twister with your partner. Who can say it faster?

» There those thousand thinkers were thinking, "How did the other three thieves go through?"

2 Vocatree

Look at the words given below, brainstorm the synonyms and antonyms for the words.

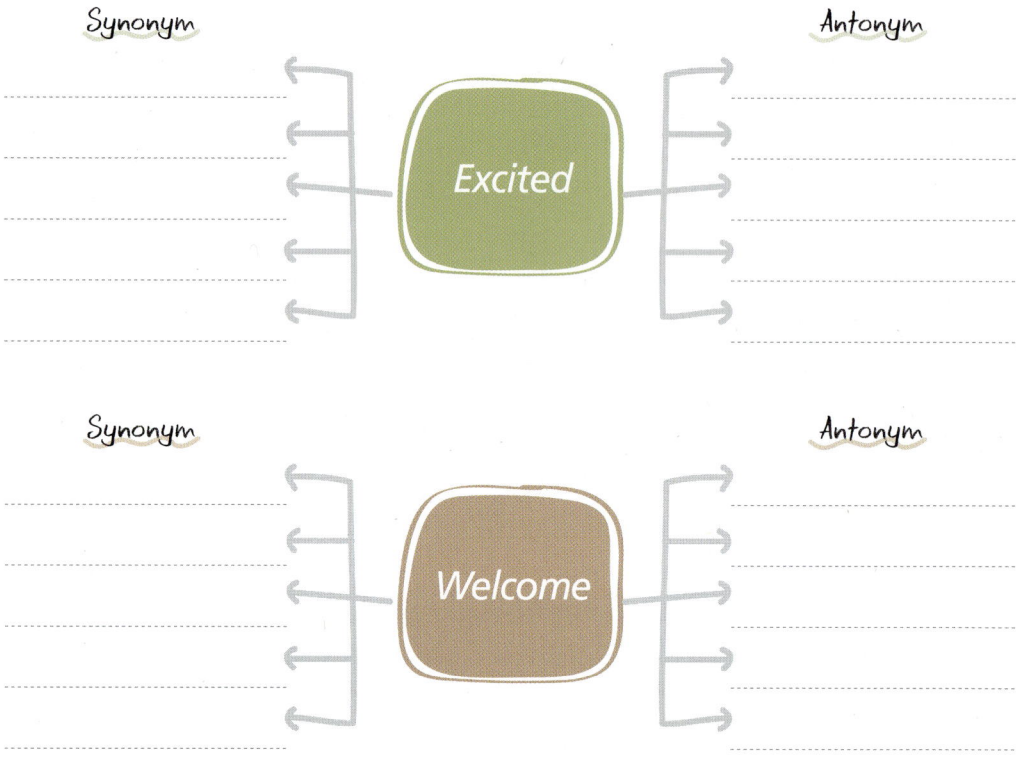

3 Sentence Building

Complete the sentences by filling in the blanks. Refer to the grammar note on the right.

1. _____ you like to come with me?
2. Why _____ we meet there?
3. Can you _____ me at the theater?
4. Would you _____ to the concert with me?
5. Would you _____ to go on vacation together?
6. Why don't you _____ to my party tonight?
7. Could _____ meet me by the door?
8. Would you like to _____ skiing?

Grammar Note

Verbs for invitations

» **Would** you **like to** have dinner with me?
» **Could** you meet me there?
» **Would** you **like to** come, too?
» **Would** you **like to** see a movie?
» **Why don't** we have dinner?

» **Could** you join me for coffee?
» **Can** you come, too?
» **Could** you call me later?
» **Would** you eat lunch with me?
» **Would** you like to go to the park?

4 Dialogue Practice

Jimmy : If you have time, would you like to go to dinner after we finish work?

Sharon : I'm sorry, but I already have dinner plans with Tim. Would you like to join us?

Jimmy : Where are you going?

Sharon : We're going to try a new Thai place.

Jimmy : That sounds enjoyable.

Sharon : It should be good. The restaurant has great reviews.

Jimmy : When are you leaving?

Sharon : We'll go around 6. I'll send you a message with directions.

Comprehension Questions

1. Why can't Sharon join Jimmy?
2. What is Jimmy and Sharon's relationship?
3. What kind of reviews might the restaurant have?

5 Story Board

Look at the situation and complete the conversation.

Situation.01

If you have time, would you like to go watch a movie with me?

Situation.02

Is your wife still out of town? Do you want to join us for dinner?

Lesson.14 Would you like to...? | 83

6 Comprehensive Listening

Listen to the dialogue and answer the questions.

A | Circle True or False

- The man and woman will go watch a movie together.   True / False
- The man's name is Sam.   True / False
- One man will eat dinner first.   True / False
- The woman might be able to go to dinner.   True / False

B | Read the following questions and write full sentence responses.

- Who is going to dinner?

- Why is the woman busy?

- What time will the movie begin?

- What time of day might the conversation take place?

7 Speaking Patterns

Practice using the patterns below with a partner.

If you have time, would you…?

» If you have time, would you like to watch a movie?
» If you have time, would you like to go to dinner?
» If you have time, would you like to go to the park?

I'm sorry, but….

» I'm sorry, but I don't have time.
» I'm sorry, but my schedule is full.
» I'm sorry, but I already made plans.

Do you want to join us for…?

» Do you want to join us for dinner?
» Do you want to join us for the movie?
» Do you want to join us for coffee?

Common Mistakes

What is correct?
Read the sentences and circle the correct answer.
Check the explanations at the back of the book.

01 He came to ask for some advice. / He came to ask for some advise.

02 I advice you to stay away from the dog. / I advise you to stay away from the dog.

03 That's my advice. / That's my advise.

8 Situational Use

What are some things you might say in each situation?

Q: What other situations can you think of? Let's think and talk some more!

9 Fun Facts

Five Smart Excuses

It has happened to everyone. You're at a business luncheon or a social gathering listening to some bore, and you would like to be anywhere else. Or, you're at a party that you'd love to stay at, but you can't. Many people are forced to stay in a situation they don't want to be in. How can we excuse ourselves or avoid the situation wisely?

01 I got lost coming here.
02 It's not an easy place to find.
03 I couldn't find a parking space.
04 I have a doctor's appointment.
05 I have a personal emergency.

Question

1. Discuss the excuses above.
   Do you think they are good excuses? Why or why not? If not, what are some good excuses?

2. Have you ever made an excuse before? Describe about the situation and the reasons for your excuse(s).

3. In what kinds of situations do you make excuses?
   Do you think making excuses is necessary? Why?

Review and Sneak Peek

Calling

_____
_____
_____
_____

Sneak Peek

01.
How often do you eat at restaurants? Who do you go with?

02.
What is your favorite food? How often do you eat it?

Lesson.14 Would you like to...? | 85

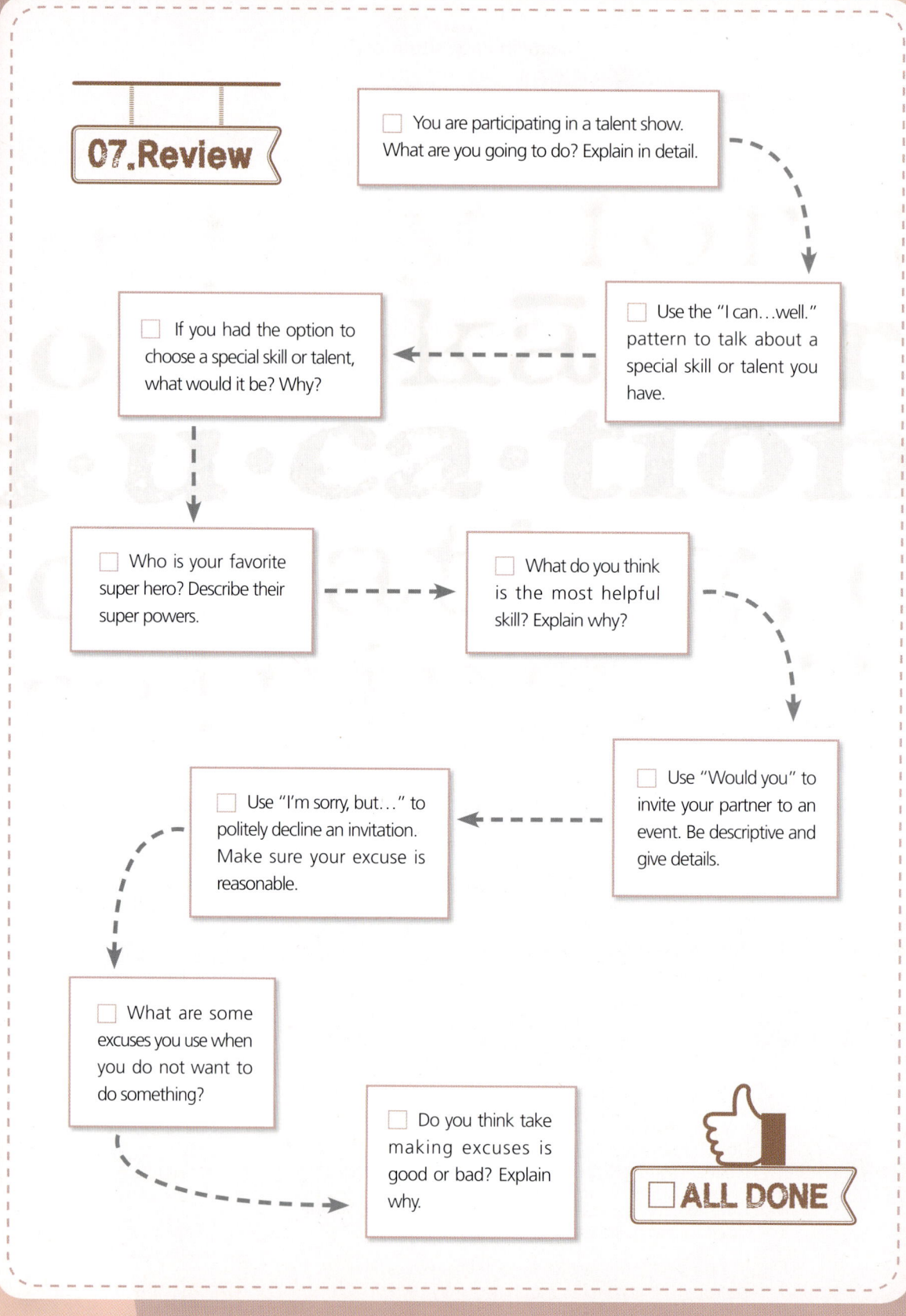

Lesson

15 Where is the menu?

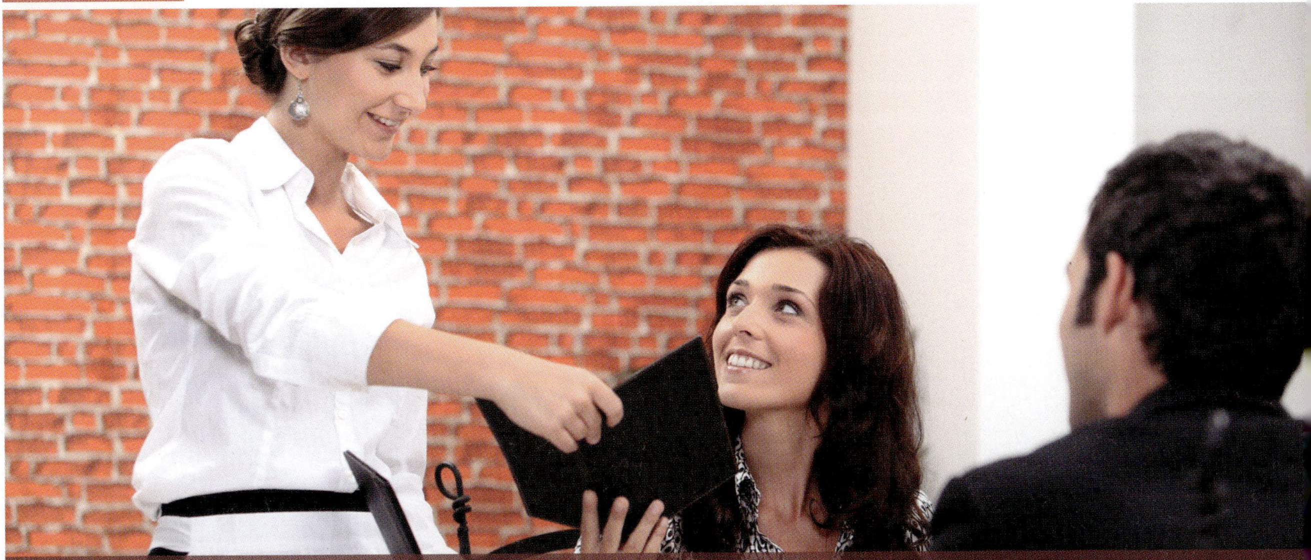

Learning Objectives : *After studying this lesson, you should be able to ...*

- ☑ order food at a restaurant
- ☑ use "I'd like" and other polite phrases accurately in a restaurant

1 Getting Started

A | Look at the picture and describe what you can see.

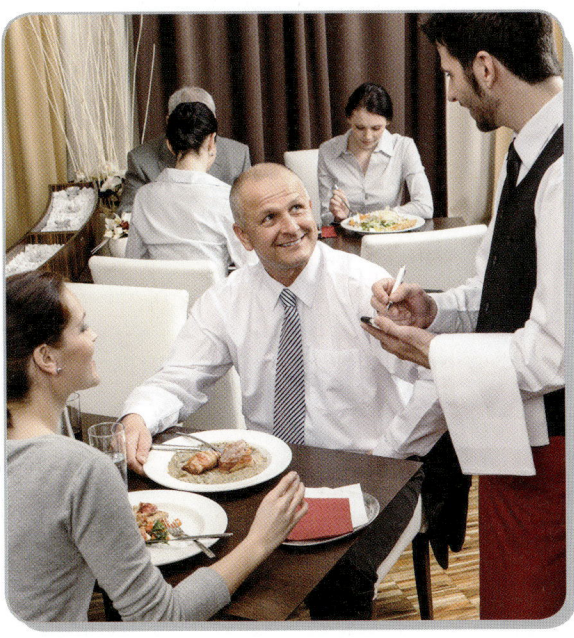

B | Read the questions below and discuss with your partner.

1. How often do you eat at a restaurant? What do you usually order?
2. What are some hot dining spots in your neighborhood? Why are they famous?

Tongue Twisters

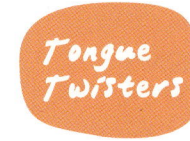

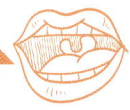

Practice the tongue twister with your partner. Who can say it faster?

» How much pot could a pot roast roast, if a pot roast could roast pot?

2 Vocatree

Look at the words given below, brainstorm the synonyms and antonyms for the words.

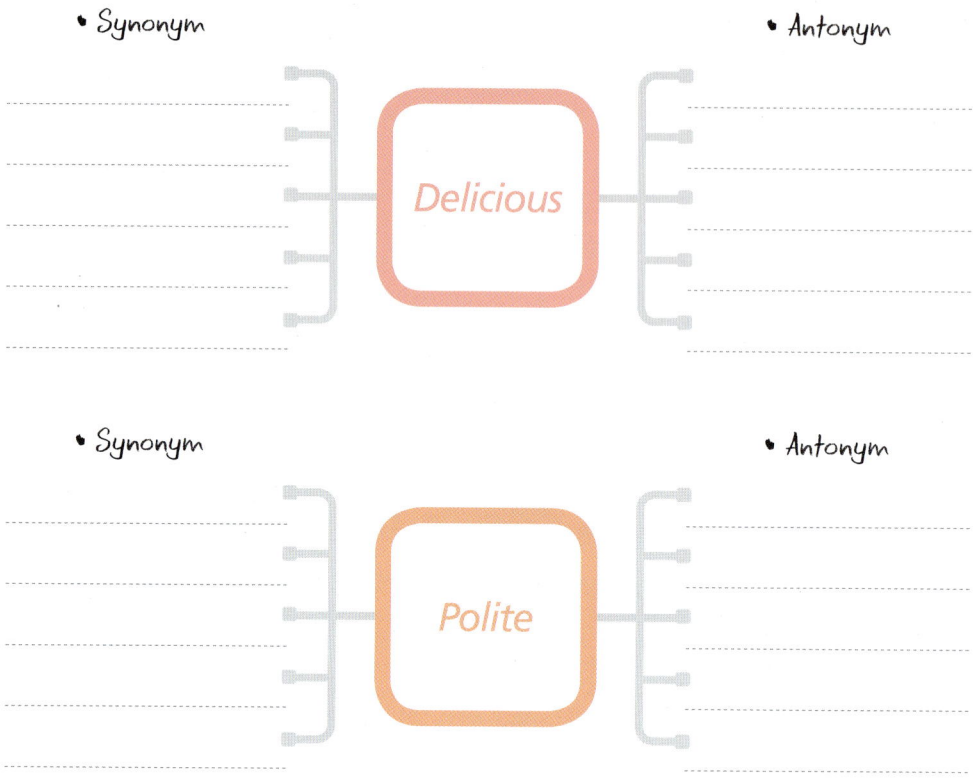

3 Sentence Building

Complete the sentences by filling in the blanks. Refer to the grammar note on the right.

1. I'd _____ toast and eggs.
2. Could you _____ me another coffee?
3. She _____ a chicken sandwich.
4. Could I _____ some beef noodles?
5. We'd _____ an order of French fries.
6. I _____ the soup.
7. _____ you bring me a menu?
8. Could I _____ some more bread?

Grammar Note

Phrases for ordering food
» **I'd like** a cheeseburger with fries.
» **Could** you **get** me a hamburger?
» **Could** I **have** the noodles?
» **She'd like** the daily special.
» **Could** you **bring** me the fried chicken?

» **Could** you **bring** me a steak?
» She **wants** the mushroom soup.
» **Could** we **have** the tomato pasta?
» **I'd like** the tofu rice.
» **I want** the fried noodles.

4 Dialogue Practice

Will : What do you feel like eating?

Sandra : I want to eat a cheeseburger.

Will : That sounds good. I might copy you. Here's the waiter.

Waiter : What can I get for you?

Will : Could I get two cheeseburgers?

Waiter : Anything else?

Sandra : Could you please refill our drinks?

Waiter : I'll be back with your drinks in a minute.

Comprehension Questions

1. Where is the conversation taking place?
2. What will come first: the food or the drinks?
3. What else do you think is on the menu? What might you order?

5 Story Board

Look at the situation and complete the conversation.

Situation.01

What can I get for you?

Situation.02

I'd like to see a menu. Also, could you refill my drink?

Lesson.15 Where is the menu? | 89

6 Comprehensive Listening

Listen to the dialogue and answer the questions.

A Circle True or False

- The woman is a waitress.   True / False
- The man ordered a drink.   True / False
- He asked for more water.   True / False
- The woman wants a sandwich.   True / False

B Read the following questions and write full sentence responses.

- What did the man order?

- Why did the man order a salad?

- What is the woman bringing first?

- What might happen next?

7 Speaking Patterns

Practice using the patterns below with a partner.

Could I get….?

» Could I get a cup of coffee?
» Could I get a hamburger?
» Could I get a sandwich?

I want to eat….

» I want to eat tomato soup.
» I want to eat French fries.
» I want to eat fried chicken.

Could you refill my…?

» Could you refill my bus card?
» Could you refill my water?
» Could you refill my tea?

Common Mistakes

What is correct?
Read the sentences and circle the correct answer.
Check the explanations at the back of the book.

01 He drinks neither wine nor beer. / He drinks neither wine or beer.

02 Would you like pasta nor salad? / Would you like pasta or salad?

03 I'm available either Friday nor Saturday. / I'm available neither Friday nor Saturday.

8 Situational Use

What are some things you might say in each situation?

Q: What other situations can you think of? Let's think and talk some more!

9 Fun Facts

Table Manners

01 | Refills and Seconds
In the Philippines and Chile, grabbing second servings on your own is not polite. You are expected to wait until the host offers you more or encourages everyone to take seconds. In China, refilling your own glass of water is also frowned upon; instead, you are supposed to fill the host's or other guests' glasses, and they will reciprocate.

02 | Clearing Your Plate
Finishing everything on your plate is considered rude in some countries, including Russia and China. Leaving some food means that your host has provided enough food, and it is an acknowledgement of your host's generosity. However, in countries like India and the Philippines, not clearing your plate is considered rude and wasteful.

03 | Belching
In China, Taiwan, and among Inuit groups in Canada, light burping is considered a compliment to the chef or host. It is the sign that you have eaten well. Conversely, in Chile and many other countries around the world, you're expected to eat quietly and neatly; belching, slurping, and other such noises are frowned upon.

Question

1. What do you think of the three table manners? Compare each with the table manners of your own country.

2. What table manners do you have, and why do you keep them?

3. Assume that you are in a different country. Ask for two or three most important table manners you need to learn. What questions will you ask?

Review and Sneak Peek

Calling
_____
_____
_____
_____

Sneak Peek

01.
How do you pay for food at a restaurant in your country? Do you need to ask for the bill or just go to the counter?

02.
Do you like dessert after a meal? Explain.

Lesson.15 Where is the menu? | 91

Lesson 16 — Shall we have some dessert?

Learning Objectives: *After studying this lesson, you should be able to …*
- ☑ order additional food and request the bill
- ☑ use countable and uncountable nouns accurately when discussing food

1 Getting Started

A | Look at the picture and describe what you can see.

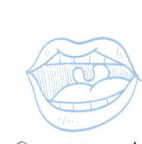 

Practice the tongue twister with your partner. Who can say it faster?

» The ruddy widow really wants ripe watermelon and red roses when winter arrives.

B | Read the questions below and discuss with your partner.

1. How do you pay for a meal when you dine with your friends?
2. On what occasions do you choose to dine at a restaurant? Why?

2 Vocatree

Look at the words given below and brainstorm the synonyms and antonyms for the words.

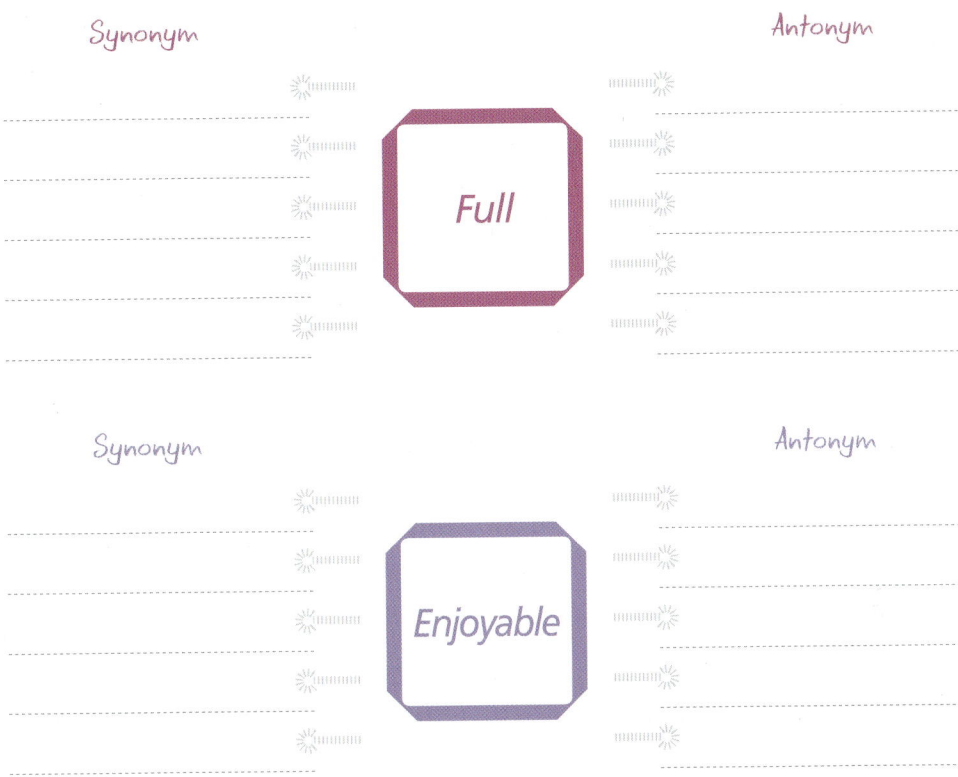

3 Sentence Building

Complete the sentences by filling in the blanks.
Refer to the grammar note on the right.

1. Give me _____ yogurt.

2. I'd like _____ cups of coffee.

3. Could I have _____ soup?

4. He wants _____ glass of water.

5. Could I have some _____ tea?

6. I want _____ chicken sandwich.

7. Could you get us three _____ of coffee?

8. We want _____ more bread.

Grammar Note

Countable nouns
Uncountable nouns

» *I'd like* **some** *milk.*
» *He wants* **a cup of** *tea.*
» *Could you give me* **a hamburger?**
» *I want* **some** *bread.*
» *Please give me* **two** *bagels.*

» *I'd like to order* **some** *soup.*
» *We need* **three bowls of** *soup.*
» *Could I have* **some more** *coffee?*
» *We'd like* **two glasses of** *coffee.*
» *Could I get* **some** *bread?*

4 Dialogue Practice

Irene : We're ready for the dessert menu.

Waiter : Okay. I'll bring it right to you.

Sandy : What do you feel like?

Irene : I'm a little full, but the chocolate cake looks so good.

Sandy : Do you want to get it to go?

Irene : We could eat it later with our coffee.

Sandy : That's a good idea.

Irene : I'd like to order a piece of cake to go, and please bring me the bill.

Waiter : Okay. I'll go put your order in.

Comprehension Questions

1. What did Irene order?
2. What might the girls have done before this conversation?
3. Why does Irene order the cake to go?

5 Story Board

Look at the situation and complete the conversation.

Situation.01

Is there anything else I can get for you?

Situation.02

I'd like to order a coffee to go.

6 Comprehensive Listening

Listen to the dialogue and answer the questions.

A Circle True or False

- The woman asks for another cup of coffee.	True / False
- The waiter gave her a menu.	True / False
- The woman liked the cake.	True / False
- She has already paid for her food.	True / False

B Read each question and write full sentence responses.

- Where did this conversation take place?

- What is the man's job?

- Why does the woman order more cake?

- What might the woman do next?

7 Speaking Patterns

Practice using the patterns below with a partner.

We're ready for….
- We're ready for the bill.
- We're ready for our main course.
- We're ready for the dessert menu.

Please bring me….
- Please bring me the menu.
- Please bring me the check.
- Please bring me some more water.

I'd like to order…to go.
- I'd like to order some more coffee to go.
- I'd like to order a sandwich to go.
- I'd like to order a piece of cake to go.

Common Mistakes

What is correct?
Read the sentences and circle the correct answer.
Check the explanations at the back of the book.

01.
Sarah's cat ran away. / Sarahs' cat ran away.

02.
The three sister's wanted to have lunch. / The three sisters' wanted to have lunch.

03.
This bathroom is for all customer's use. / This bathroom is for all customers' use.

Lesson.16 Shall we have some dessert?

8 Situational Use

What are some things you might say in each situation?

Q: What other situations can you think of? Let's think and talk some more!

9 Fun Facts

Sweet Delirium

- **Chocolate Soufflé with Grand Marnier (France)** Chocolate soufflé is a lightly baked cake made of egg yolks, beaten egg whites, sugar, and a gooey chocolate interior. In France, it is often infused with Grand Marnier, orange liquor.

- **Apple Pie (United States)** Apple pie is an American dessert which consists of a pastry pie crust and an apple filling often seasoned with nutmeg or cinnamon. It does not originate from the United States but was brought over by the Pilgrims from England.

- **Gelato (Italy)** Gelato differs from ice cream in its flavor and texture. The frozen dessert is made with milk as opposed to cream, and has less air whipped into it than ice cream, making it denser and often more intense in flavor. Gelato is an Italian term that means "frozen."

- **Babka (Poland)** Babka is a Polish dish which is like a sweet cake with a spongy texture. It is usually filled with fruits like raisins. "Babka" is a Polish word which means "grandmother."

- **Basbousa (Egypt)** Basbousa is an Egyptian street food and is a semi-sweet cake often topped with lime curd, whipped cream, and berries.

- **Alfajores (Argentina)** This Latin American treat is a popular in Argentina. The word "alfajor" is rooted in the Arab word for "honeycomb." They are often served with coffee and traditionally dipped in chocolate, though "snow alfajores" are dipped in powdered sugar and coconut.

Question

❶ Do you usually have dessert after a meal? Why or why not?

❷ After a satisfactory meal, what would you order for dessert? How much do you expect on your bill for the dessert?

❸ Share your favorite dessert. Explain the ingredients, tastes, feelings, and price.

Review and Sneak Peek

Calling

_____
_____
_____
_____

Sneak Peek

01.
What things do you usually talk about when meeting an old friend?

03.
How has your life changed in the past year?

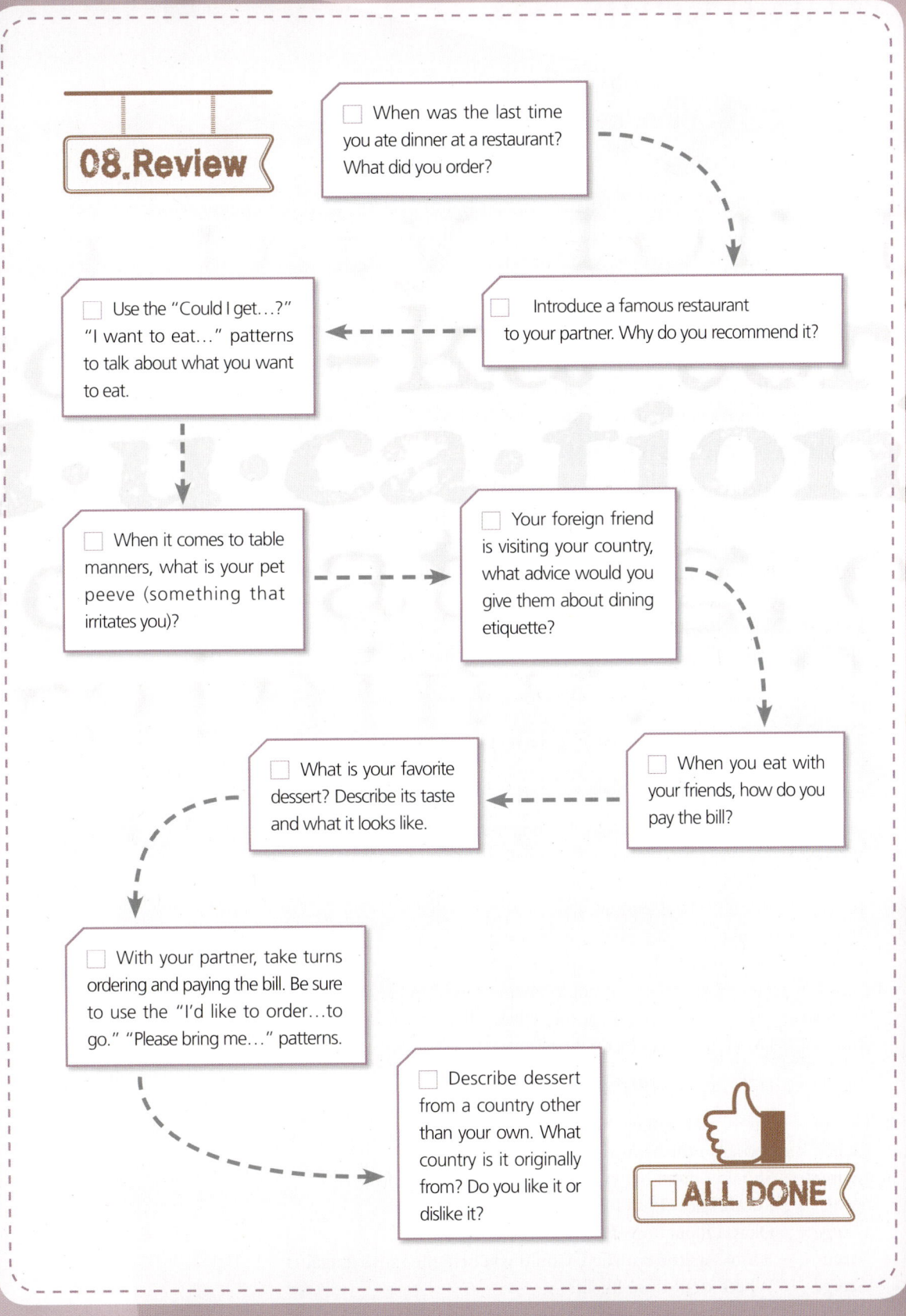

AUDIO SCRIPTS

Lesson.01 A new neighborhood

DIALOGUE PRACTICE

Sam : Hello! Are you new to the neighborhood? I haven't seen you around before.
John : Yes, I am new here. My family moved here yesterday.
Sam : Great! Nice to meet you. I'm Sam.
John : My name's John. This is my family. My wife's name is Suzie, and this is my son, Zach.
Sam : It's a pleasure to meet you. Are you from LA?
John : No, we are from Washington.
Sam : Really? Have you met the Johnsons? They are from Washington, too. Well, we live next door. If you need any help, feel free to come over.
John : Thanks very much.

COMPREHENSIVE LISTENING

John : Hello, Sam. Nice to see you again.
Sam : Hi, John. Have you met the Johnsons? This is Mary.
Mary : Hello, nice to meet you. I'm Mary Johnson. Are you new to this area?
John : Yes, my family moved here from Washington.
Mary : I'm from Washington, too!
John : Have you lived here for a long time?
Mary : No, only a year, but feel free to ask for any help!
John : Thanks, I appreciate it.

Lesson.02 Where can I put this?

DIALOGUE PRACTICE

May : Thank you so much for helping me move.
Susanna : No problem. I'm always happy to help.
May : Where does this box go?
Susanna : Put it in the bedroom.
May : Could you help me move the sofa?
Susanna : Sure. Where should we put it?
May : I'm not sure. How about the living room? What do you think?
Susanna : I think it would look good between the two tables.
May : Good idea. Let's move it on three.

COMPREHENSIVE LISTENING

George : Sarah, where does this desk go?
Sarah : It goes in the bedroom.
George : Should I put it between your bed and the window.
Sarah : I don't know Dad. I think by the door is better.
George : Okay, I'll put it over there.
Sarah : It looks a little crowded. Could you help me move it again?
George : Where would you like it?
Sarah : Can we put it between the bed and the window?

Lesson.03 It's a house warming party

DIALOGUE PRACTICE

Jane	: Thank you for inviting us to your housewarming party, Alex.
Emily	: Your new home is lovely, and everything looks so modern.
Alex	: I'm just happy you came. Would you like a drink?
Jane	: Just some water, please.
Emily	: I'm impressed by the view.
Alex	: Yes, it's my favorite part, too.
Jane	: Could you tell me more about why you moved?
Alex	: Well, I'm actually closer to my work now.

COMPREHENSIVE LISTENING

Colin	: I love your new place! I'm impressed by the location.
Jessica	: It's nice, isn't it?
Colin	: Yes, it has a lovely night view, too.
Jessica	: Would you like a tour?
Colin	: Yes, tell me more about the apartment.
Jessica	: Well, it has three bedrooms, and each has a very nice view of the city.
Colin	: How many bathrooms do you have?
Jessica	: Just one bathroom. It's right here.

Lesson.04 This is my favorite song!

DIALOGUE PRACTICE

Marianne	: What did you think of the movie?
Sam	: I loved it. I thought it was great!
Marianne	: It was such a fun movie.
Sam	: The ending was a big surprise. It was so exciting.
Marianne	: I thought so, too.
Sam	: I think it is my new favorite movie.
Marianne	: Did you enjoy the main actor's performance?
Sam	: I thought he was amazing!

COMPREHENSIVE LISTENING

Daniel	: Thank you for inviting me last night.
Claire	: It was my pleasure. What did you think of the party?
Daniel	: I thought it was great! Normally, I dislike big parties, but yours was very fun.
Claire	: That's good to hear.
Daniel	: The food was so delicious.
Claire	: Thanks! I made it all myself.
Daniel	: Really? Did you make the chicken, too?
Claire	: Yes, I did. Did you enjoy it?
Daniel	: It was perfect!

AUDIO SCRIPTS

Lesson.05 You look tired

DIALOGUE PRACTICE

Andrew   : Hi Michelle, how was your weekend? Did you see Carol?
Michelle : Yes, I saw her after work. We met for dinner.
Andrew   : What did you eat?
Michelle : We went to a nice Italian restaurant.
Andrew   : That sounds like fun.
Michelle : The food was so good! Do you like pasta?
Andrew   : Yes, I do.
Michelle : We should go there together next time.

COMPREHENSIVE LISTENING

Richard : Hey, Amanda! I haven't seen you in a while.
Amanda : I just got back from a vacation in Spain.
Richard : How was your vacation? Did you like Spain?
Amanda : It was great. I really enjoyed it. You look tired today.
Richard : Yeah, I met a friend after work yesterday.
Amanda : Really? What did you do?
Richard : We met for dinner and watched a movie. Now I'm really tired.
Amanda : You should go home early tonight.

Lesson.06 I'm running late

DIALOGUE PRACTICE

Mark : What time is your dentist appointment tomorrow?
Anna : It's at 8 A.M. I'm worried I'll be late for it.
Mark : I think you should set your alarm extra early.
Anna : That's a good idea.
Mark : When do you think your appointment will finish?
Anna : I think it will take about an hour.
Mark : That's not bad. Do you want me to wait for you?
Anna : That would be great. Thanks.

COMPREHENSIVE LISTENING

Allen : What time is our flight tomorrow?
Lyn   : I think it leaves around 3 in the afternoon.
Allen : When should we leave for the airport?
Lyn   : Let's see … we have to get there two hours early … and I think it will take 90 minutes to get there.
Allen : Okay. Let's leave at 11:30.
Lyn   : Let's leave a little earlier than that. There might be traffic. I'm worried we might be late.
Allen : That sounds good.
Lyn   : We don't want to miss our flight.

Lesson.07 What are you doing?

DIALOGUE PRACTICE

Christopher	:	Are you doing anything tonight?
Jennifer	:	We were thinking of going to a movie.
Kathleen	:	Do you want to come along? I'm just booking the tickets right now.
Christopher	:	When are you going?
Jennifer	:	We're leaving at 7.
Christopher	:	I'm a little busy with work now, but I think I will finish soon.
Kathleen	:	Give us a call if you can come.
Jennifer	:	I really hope you can make it.
Christopher	:	Okay. Talk to you soon.

COMPREHENSIVE LISTENING

Lyn	:	Where are you going? Are you doing anything special tonight?
Allen	:	I'm just getting ready to go home.
Lyn	:	Did you eat yet?
Allen	:	No, I was going to eat at home.
Lyn	:	I was going to eat out tonight. Do you want to get something to eat together?
Allen	:	I have time if you want. When are you leaving?
Lyn	:	Right now. I'll just go get my bag.
Allen	:	Okay. I'll wait by the elevator.

Lesson.08 Let me check my schedule

DIALOGUE PRACTICE

Robert	:	Hey, Stan! It's been a long time!
Stan	:	What are you doing here at the park?
Robert	:	I often take a walk here during my lunch break.
Stan	:	How have you been lately?
Robert	:	I've been pretty busy with work. What are you doing this weekend?
Stan	:	We are planning to go camping this weekend.
Robert	:	Do you want to plan to get dinner sometime? I always eat near here after work.
Stan	:	That sounds good. Give me a call.

COMPREHENSIVE LISTENING

Grace	:	Hey, Johnny! I didn't know you were a member of this gym. I've never seen you before.
Peter	:	Oh, I always go to the gym after work.
Grace	:	I usually come in the morning.
Peter	:	What are you doing on Saturday? We are having a party this weekend.
Grace	:	I'm busy with work this weekend.
Peter	:	How about meeting for lunch next week?
Grace	:	That sounds good.
Peter	:	I often eat out during my lunch break.
Grace	:	Okay. I'll give you a call.

Audio Scripts

AUDIO SCRIPTS

Lesson.09　Going to work

DIALOGUE PRACTICE

David   : It's great seeing you again. What do you do now?
Susie   : I work as a receptionist, but I don't like it much. In the future, I'd like to do what my husband does.
David   : What does he do?
Susie   : He works as an accountant.
David   : Isn't it a difficult job?
Susie   : Yes, but his work seems interesting. My current job is not challenging enough.
David   : I can understand that. My job is a little boring at times.
Susie   : Really? What do you do?

COMPREHENSIVE LISTENING

Marcus   : What have you been doing since graduation?
Melanie : I work as a nurse at a clinic now. How about you?
Marcus   : I'm working in an office, but I'd like to change jobs.
Melanie : What do you want to do?
Marcus   : In the future, I'd like to work for my father's company.
Melanie : What does your father do? I forgot…
Marcus   : He runs a chain of restaurants. He wants to expand it abroad.
Melanie : That sounds like a good opportunity.

Lesson.10　Weekend plans

DIALOGUE PRACTICE

Margaret : What are your plans for the weekend?
Eric   : This weekend, I'm going to a jazz music festival.
Margaret : That sounds like so much fun! Where is it?
Eric   : It's going to be held at Olympic Park. Do you want to go?
Margaret : I think I have to work on Saturday, but I'm not sure yet.
Eric   : It would be great if you could make it.
Margaret : Tonight, I will check my schedule and let you know.
Eric   : Okay. Let me know. If you can go, I will get a ticket for you.

COMPREHENSIVE LISTENING

Tony   : This weekend, I'm going to play soccer with my co-workers.
Joanna : That sounds like fun. What time will you come home?
Tony   : I should be back around 1.
Joanna : Will you eat with them?
Tony   : I don't think so.
Joanna : Okay, I will have lunch ready for you. We can eat together.
Tony   : Sounds like a plan. Have you seen my sports bag?
Joanna : I washed it last night. It should be dry before the weekend.

Lesson.11 These are my hobbies

DIALOGUE PRACTICE

Amanda : Do you have any hobbies?
Jason : I enjoy horseback riding in my free time. Have you ever tried it?
Amanda : I tried it on my last vacation, but I didn't like it much.
Jason : Oh no, why?
Amanda : Honestly, I was a little scared of being on such a big animal. It was my first time.
Jason : You probably just need more practice. I find horseback riding a lot of fun.
Amanda : Maybe I could go with you sometime.
Jason : That would be fun.

COMPREHENSIVE LISTENING

Angela : What do you usually do on the weekend?
Collin : I like to go camping in my free time.
Angela : That sounds like fun. I've never been. What do you do when you camp?
Collin : I usually go fishing and swimming, too.
Angela : I love fishing! I find it very relaxing. What kind of fish do you catch?
Collin : Have you ever tried rainbow trout?
Angela : I tried it on vacation once. It was delicious.
Collin : I'll bring you back some the next time I go.

Lesson.12 I've been playing for a while

DIALOGUE PRACTICE

Mrs. Bell : I can't believe how well you and your brother play!
Rosie : Thank you. I'm glad you liked the song.
Mrs. Bell : How long have you been learning?
Rosie : I've been playing the piano since I was 12 years old … and my brother has been playing guitar for almost 15 years.
Bob : It hasn't been that long, has it? I've been playing since I was 12.
Rosie : And you're 27 now, so 15 years.
Bob : I guess my sister is right. It doesn't feel like it's been that long.
Mrs. Bell : Anyway, you're both very talented musicians. Could you play me another song?

COMPREHENSIVE LISTENING

Kayden : You play the flute very well.
Agnes : Thank you. I have played it since I was 14 years old. Do you play any instruments?
Kayden : I play the cello.
Agnes : I hear that's really difficult.
Kayden : I like it, though. I've been playing since I was in high school.
Agnes : I'd love to hear you play sometime.
Kayden : I have a concert next week.
Agnes : Really? You'll have to tell me the details.

AUDIO SCRIPTS

Lesson.13 Can you? Can't you?

DIALOGUE PRACTICE

Dan   : Are you ready to leave?
Grace   : Not yet. Just a few more minutes.
Dan   : What are you doing?
Grace   : I have to reply to a few e-mails for work. I have to write in Spanish.
Dan   : When will you be able to finish? We'll be late for the movie.
Grace   : It shouldn't take long. I can write Spanish well.
Dan   : Okay. I'll wait in the car.
Grace   : I'll be ready soon. Don't worry.

COMPREHENSIVE LISTENING

Christy : How did you learn this computer program?
Joshua : I have to use it for data entry at work.
Christy : You're so fast. When will you be able to help me learn?
Joshua : I'm busy now…. I have to finish this project for work today.
Christy : How about next weekend?
Joshua : That sounds good.
Christy : Do you want to come over for dinner? I can cook well.
Joshua : I'd like that.

Lesson.14 Would you like to…?

DIALOGUE PRACTICE

Jimmy   : If you have time, would you like to go to dinner after we finish work?
Sharon : I'm sorry, but I already have dinner plans with Tim. Would you like to join us?
Jimmy   : Where are you going?
Sharon : We're going to try a new Thai place.
Jimmy   : That sounds enjoyable.
Sharon : It should be good. The restaurant has great reviews.
Jimmy   : When are you leaving?
Sharon : We'll go around 6. I'll send you a message with directions.

COMPREHENSIVE LISTENING

Patrick : If you have time, would you like to watch a movie tonight?
Regina : That sounds like fun. When are you going?
Patrick : The movie starts at 8, but I'm meeting Sam for dinner first. Do you want to join us?
Regina : I'm sorry, but I have a lot of work to finish.
Patrick : That's too bad.
Regina : I might be able to make the movie, but not dinner.
Patrick : Just let me know later.
Regina : Okay. Have a nice lunch.

Lesson.15 Where is the menu?

DIALOGUE PRACTICE

Will	:	What do you feel like eating?
Sandra	:	I want to eat a cheeseburger.
Will	:	That sounds good. I might copy you. Here's the waiter.
Waiter	:	What can I get for you?
Will	:	Could I get two cheeseburgers?
Waiter	:	Anything else?
Sandra	:	Could you please refill our drinks?
Waiter	:	I'll be back with your drinks in a minute.

COMPREHENSIVE LISTENING

Waitress	:	Are you ready to order?
Jonathan	:	Could I get a chicken salad sandwich?
Waitress	:	Would you like any sides?
Jonathan	:	I want to eat something light. Do you have salads?
Waitress	:	Yes, we do. Should I bring you one?
Jonathan	:	Yes, please, and could you refill my water?
Waitress	:	Of course. I'll bring it right to you.
Jonathan	:	Thank you.

Lesson.16 Shall we have some dessert?

DIALOGUE PRACTICE

Irene	:	We're ready for the dessert menu.
Waiter	:	Okay. I'll bring it right to you.
Sandy	:	What do you feel like?
Irene	:	I'm a little full, but the chocolate cake looks so good.
Sandy	:	Do you want to get it to go?
Irene	:	We could eat it later with our coffee.
Sandy	:	That's a good idea.
Irene	:	I'd like to order a piece of cake to go, and please bring me the bill.
Waiter	:	Okay. I'll go put your order in.

COMPREHENSIVE LISTENING

Waiter	:	Is there anything else I can get for you?
Alice	:	Yes, I'm ready for the dessert menu.
Waiter	:	Just a minute.
Alice	:	Please bring me some coffee and a piece of cake.
Waiter	:	Here you are.
Alice	:	That cake was amazing! I'd like to order another piece to go.
Waiter	:	Okay. I'll get that ready for you.
Alice	:	Also, please bring me the bill.

COMMON MISTAKES

Lesson.01

Answers

1. The woman wanted to buy an umbrella.
2. The student wanted to work at an NGO.
3. There is a university in the city.

Explanation

a vs an

If the word following begins with a vowel sound, the word you should use is *an*.
If the word following begins with a consonant, but begins with a vowel sound, you still need to use *an*.
When the following word definitely begins with a consonant sound, you use *a*.
Note that the letter Y can be either a vowel or a consonant. Words beginning with the letter U which start with a Y consonant sound like "university" and "utensil" also use *a*. But when an initial U has a vowel sound, the word is preceded by *an*, such as "an umpire," "an umbrella," and "an understanding."

Lesson.02

Answers

1. That apple looks delicious. Could you pass me the apple?
2. The children can be very naughty.
3. Milk is sold in the supermarket.

Explanation

a vs the

Articles are used before nouns. If the noun is countable and singular it must almost always be preceded by an article (or some other 'determiner', such as this, his etc).
The is the definite article, which means that it is used when the writer expects that the reader knows which particular thing or person the writer is referring to. *The* is almost always used with superlatives, and with words such as first, last and only: The is not used with possessives
A is the indefinite article and is used when things or people are referred to which are not already known to the reader. It is used with singular, countable nouns.
When we are talking about things or people in general, *the* is not normally used if the noun is plural or uncountable.

Lesson.03

Answers

1. James and I are going fishing.
2. I bought the coffee at a café.
3. My friends and I want to eat pasta.

Explanation

I / me / my

I is used as a subject of a sentence.
Me is used as the object of a verb or preposition.
My is a possessive adjective.

Lesson.04

Answers

1. They gave us the prize.
2. Our mothers and we are going shopping.
3. We boys will go for a swim.

Explanation

we vs us

We is a subject form.
Us an object.
Simply, we do things and things are done to or for us.

PRE GET UP TO SPEED 1
ANSWER KEY

Lesson.05

Answers

1. Your writing will improve if you practice.
2. I hope you're feeling better.
3. You're late today.

Explanation

your vs you're

Your is a possessive adjective.
You're is always a contraction of "you are."

Hint : If you've written "you're," try substituting "you are." If it doesn't work, the word you want is "your."

Lesson.06

Answers

1. Do you know who's going to speak?
2. I know a woman whose children study there.
3. Whose side are you on?

Explanation

who's vs whose

Who's is a contraction of "who is" or, less commonly, "who has."
Whose is the possessive of "who" or, somewhat controversially, "which."

Lesson.07

Answers

1. You can set up your own bank account.
2. The entire situation was a setup.
3. She wanted to set up the television in the bedroom.

Explanation

set up vs setup

Noun forms are most commonly one-word forms.
Phrasal verbs are generally two words.
Setup in its one-word form is a noun.
Set up is a two word phrasal verb.
If the word involved is immediately preceded by "a," "an," or "the," you probably need the one-word noun form. If it's immediately preceded by "to," you probably need the two-word phrasal verb.

Lesson.08

Answers

1. They're ready to go home.
2. There is no one in the library.
3. Their office is near the police station.

Explanation

they're / their / there

They're is always a contraction of "there are."
Their is a possessive pronoun.
There is usually used as an adverb but can also be used as a pronoun, noun, adjective, and interjection.

Hint : "there" has "here" buried inside it to remind you it refers to place, while "their" has "heir" buried in it to remind you that it has to do with possession.

Common mistakes

COMMON MISTAKES

Lesson.09

Answers

1. This book is good.
2. You speak English well.
3. Did the movie do well at the box office?

Explanation

good vs well

Good is an adjective that modifies nouns.
Good can be used with copular verbs (verbs which express a state of being, such as to be, to seem, and to appear), but it is still an adjective modifying a noun, not a verb.
Well is an adverb that modifies verbs, adjectives, and other adverbs.
Well can also be used as an adjective to mean "in good health."

Lesson.10

Answers

1. The book has lost many of its pages.
2. It's not cold enough to wear a coat.
3. She told me that it's time for bed.

Explanation

its vs it's

Its is a possessive pronoun. It is an exception to the general rule that one should use an apostrophe to indicate possession is in possessive pronouns.
It's is the contraction of "it is" or "it has."

Lesson.11

Answers

1. Lisa is the girl with whom I'm driving to the beach.
2. Jack is the one who wants to eat pizza.
3. This is the doctor whom I told you about.

Explanation

who vs whom

Who is an interrogative pronoun and is used in place of the subject of a question.
Who can also be used in statements, in place of the subject of a clause.
Whom is also an interrogative pronoun, but it is used in place of the object of a question.
And *whom* can be used in statements, in place of the object of a clause. *Whom* is always the correct choice after a preposition.

Lesson.12

Answers

1. She was tired too.
2. There were two birds on the tree.
3. I want to visit the museum.

Explanation

to / too / two

To is the most common form. When "to" is used before a verb it forms part of the infinitive. It is also a preposition, often used to indicate direction, which begins a prepositional phrase.
Too is an adverb meaning "extra or more than necessary." It can also mean "also."
Two is a number - 2.

PRE GET UP TO SPEED 1
ANSWER KEY

Lesson.13

Answers

1. He went into the army.
2. The girl dived back in to rescue the drowning boy.
3. The council is looking into the scandal.

Explanation

into vs in to

Into is a preposition which often answers the question, "where?"
In to appears when the two the words "in" and "to" just happen to find themselves neighbors, they must remain separate words.

Lesson.14

Answers

1. He came to ask for some advice.
2. I advise you to stay away from the dog.
3. That's my advice.

Explanation

advice vs advise

Advice is a noun and refers to information offered by one person to another to help the latter make a decision or take action.
Advise is a verb and means to offer a suggestion about what to do.

Lesson.15

Answers

1. He drinks neither wine nor beer.
2. Would you like pasta or salad?
3. I'm not available neither Friday nor Saturday.

Explanation

nor vs or

nor is a conjunction always used in the negative, usually before the second or last of a set of negative possibilities, we use it after 'neither'.
or is a conjunction used to connect different possibilities.

Hint: If you don't use "neither" you can use "or."

Lesson.16

Answers

1. Sarah's cat ran away.
2. The three sisters' wanted to have lunch.
3. This bathroom is for all customers' use.

Explanation

Apostrophe use

Apostrophe followed by S is used to indicate possession. However, the position of the apostrophe before or after the S depends on whether the word is a plural form ending in S. If there is an indication of possession to a plural form ending with S, the apostrophe is added to the end of the word without an additional S. If the word ending with S is singular, both an apostrophe and S must be added.

Common mistakes | 109